Houghton Mifflin Harcourt

PERFORMANCE ASSESSMENT

5

Cover and Title Page Photo Credit: ©imagewerks/Getty Images

Printed in the U.S.A.

ISBN 978-0-544-46519-0

22 0877 19

4500788495 A B C D E F G

Welcome Students,

The more you practice something, the better you get at it. With *Performance Assessment*, you will have the chance to practice reading and writing

- **opinion essays**
- **informative essays**
- **literary analysis**
- **narratives**

In each unit, you will master one of these types of writing by following three simple steps.

- **Analyze the Model**
- **Practice the Task**
- **Perform the Task**

As you follow these steps, you'll find yourself building the confidence you need to succeed at performance assessments. Let's get started!

Unit 1 Opinion Essay
School: What Works?

Step 1 • Analyze the Model

Do we need school libraries?

Read Source Materials

Step 2 • Practice the Task

Is art class important?

Read Source Materials

Write an Opinion Essay

Step 3 • Perform the Task

How much homework should teachers assign?

Read Source Materials

Write an Opinion Essay

Unit 2 Informative Essay
Early American Heroes

Step 1 • Analyze the Model

What made Ann Bailey a hero?

Read Source Materials

Step 2 • Practice the Task

What led Tecumseh to fight?

Read Source Materials

Step 3 • Perform the Task

How did York's life change after his adventure?

Read Source Materials

Unit 3 Response to Literature
The Way I See It

Step 1 • Analyze the Model

How do characters interact in a story?

Step 2 • Practice the Task

How does point of view influence the way events are described?

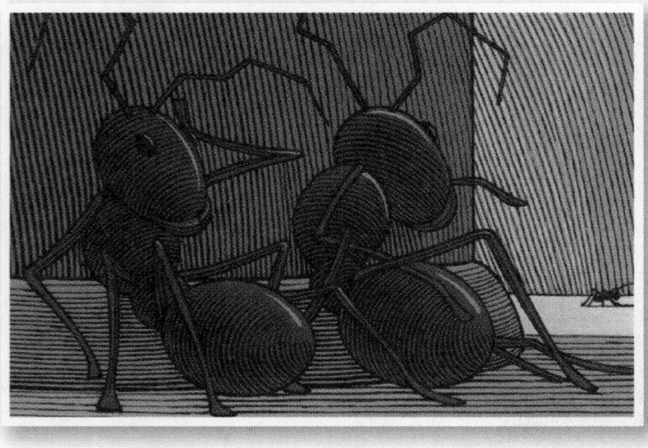

Step 3 • Perform the Task

How can a narrator shape the way events are presented?

Read Source Materials

Unit 4 Narrative
Surprising Meetings

Step 1 • Analyze the Model

What happens when Houdini meets Einstein?

Read Source Materials

Step 2 • Practice the Task

What happens when superheroes compete at a field day?

Read Source Materials

Write a Narrative

Step 3 • Perform the Task

What happens when you realize you are not alone in a strange house?

Read Source Materials

Write a Narrative

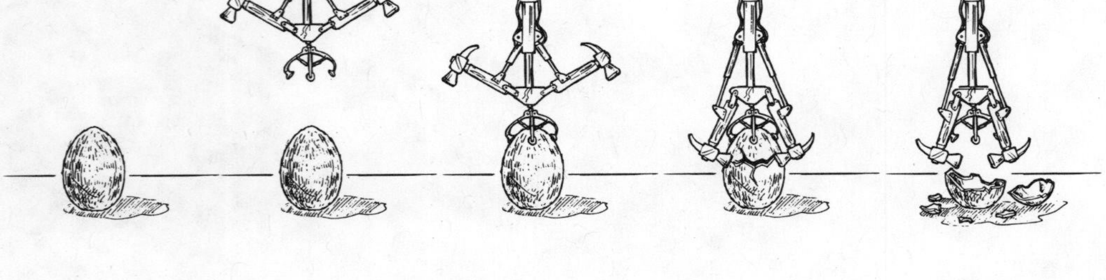

Unit 5 Mixed Practice
On Your Own

Task 1 • Opinion Essay
Research Simulation

Task 2 • Informative Essay
Research Simulation

Task 3 • Response to Literature

Task 4 • Narrative
Research Simulation

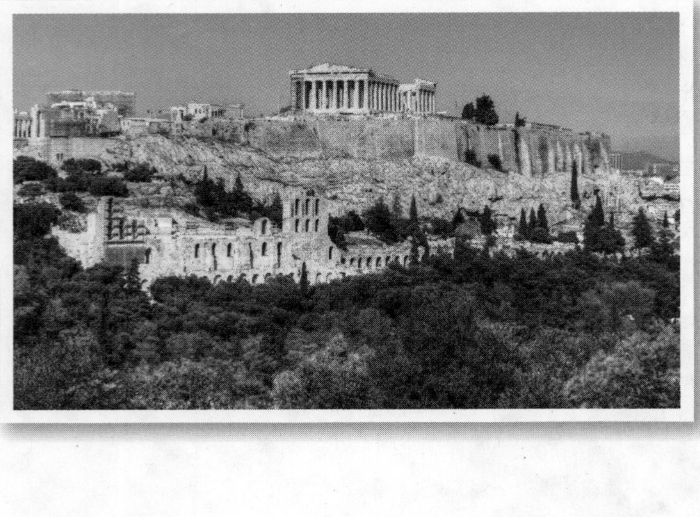

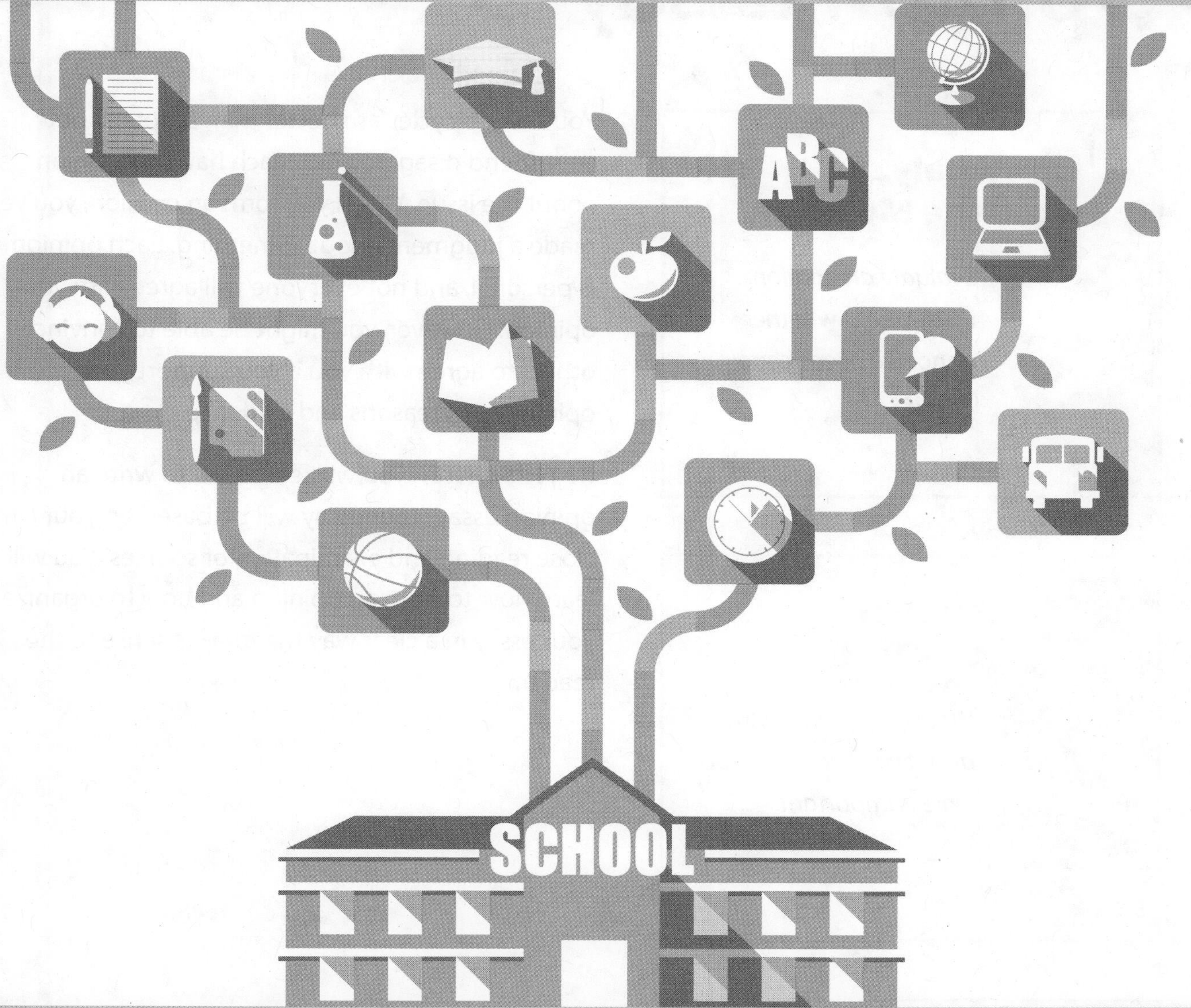

School: What Works?

Unit 1

Opinion Essay

Step 1

Analyze the Model

Evaluate an opinion essay about whether or not we need school libraries.

Step 2

Practice the Task

Write an opinion essay about whether or not art class is important.

Step 3

Perform the Task

Write an opinion essay about how much homework teachers should assign.

You think bicycles are better than scooters, but your friend disagrees. You each have an opinion about the issue. When you form an opinion, you've made a judgment about something. Each opinion is personal, and not everyone will agree with your opinion. However, you might be able to convince others to agree with you if you support your opinion with reasons and evidence.

IN THIS UNIT, you will learn how to write an opinion essay. Your essay will be based on your close reading and examination of sources. You will learn how to state an opinion and how to organize your essay in a clear way that makes sense to the reader.

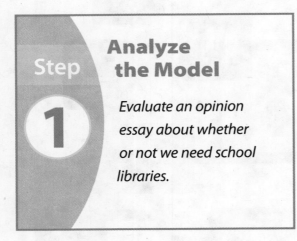

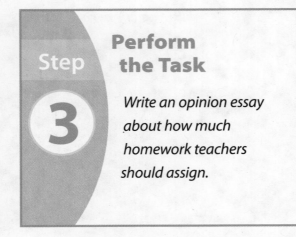

Step 1 Analyze the Model

Do we need school libraries?

You will read:

- **An Invitation**
  Support Our Shelves!
- **A Survey**
  Survey of eBook Use in School Libraries, 2012

You will analyze:

- **A Student Model**
  Libraries Teach Us How to Think

Source 1: Invitation

This invitation was used by Mr. Plausky's student, Nahee Chung, as one of the sources for her essay, "Libraries Teach Us How to Think." As you read, make notes in the side columns. Underline information that you find useful.

Notes

Support Our Shelves!

A Family Dinner to Benefit

The Holton Elementary Library Renovation

June 18th • 6PM

At the Roosevelt Civic Center

We hope you will join us during graduation week for a very special event to help us bring the Holton Elementary School Library into the twenty-first century. For the last forty years, our collection has educated, informed, and entertained generations of students. We are committed to teaching children how to locate and evaluate information. We believe that these skills will stay with them for a lifetime.

Notes

With your generous donations, the Children's Room will be expanded and improved, adding more space for books and a third librarian station. New technology upgrades will feature brand-new computer stations and a tablet-lending station for older students. Upstairs, a new Community Room will also be used as a meeting room. The library will meet safety requirements for full occupancy with the installation of a second staircase at the back of the building.

That is a good book which is opened with expectation and closed with profit. —Amos Bronson Alcott

Please RSVP no later than May 1.

We are grateful for your donations.

Discuss and Decide

What services will the Holton Elementary Library offer students?

Source 2: Survey

Nahee used this survey as a second source for her essay. Continue to make notes in the side columns as you read. Underline information that you find helpful.

Notes

Survey of eBook Use in School Libraries, 2012

In 2012, a survey of U.S. school libraries was done to determine their use of eBooks. Of the 1,427 schools that participated in the survey, 942 were elementary schools. Compared to public and academic libraries, school libraries are behind in the adoption of eBooks. The number of eBook titles per student is one way to see how well a library may be keeping up with trends and technology. A ratio of one eBook per student would be considered competitive.

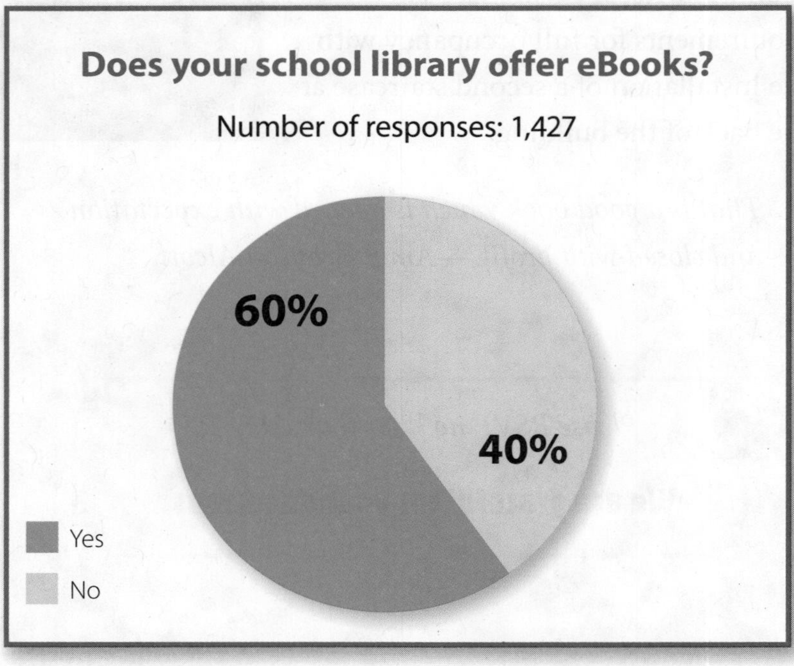

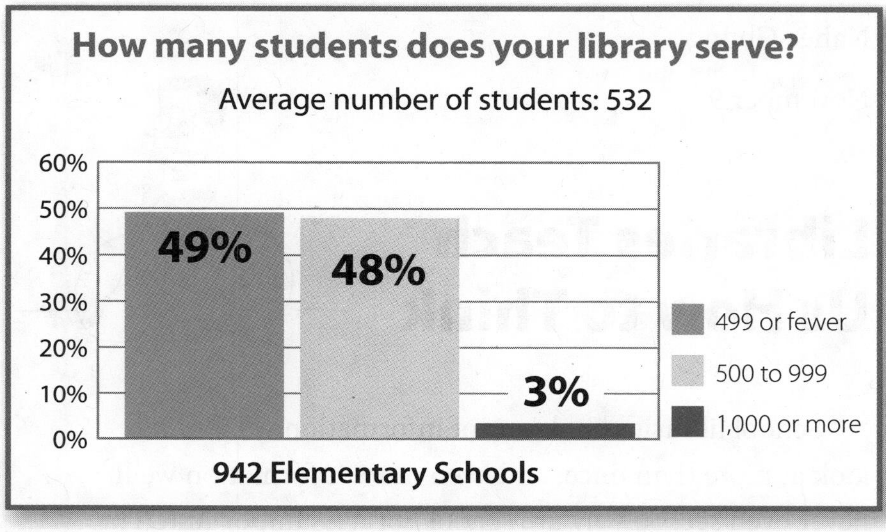

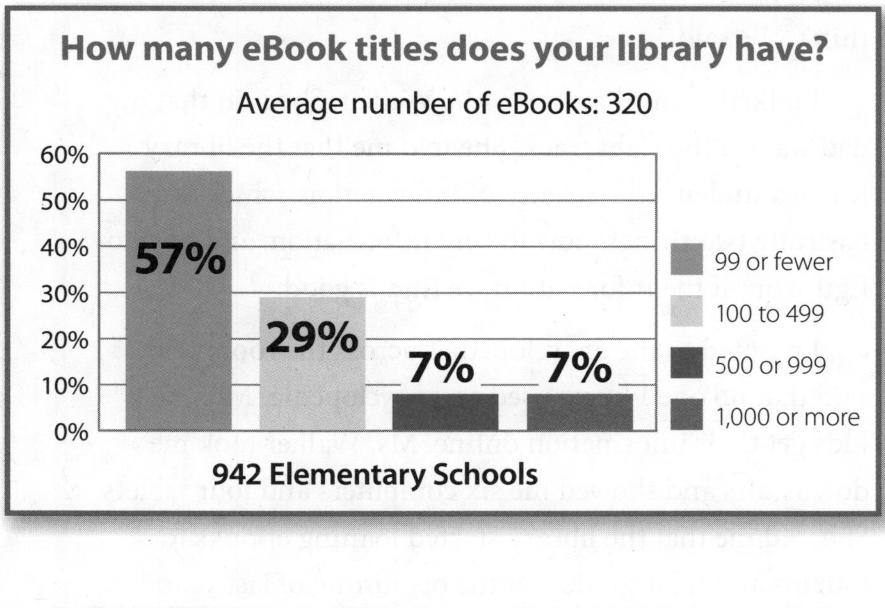

Discuss and Decide

You have read two sources about school libraries. Without reading any further, discuss the question: Do we need school libraries?

Notes

Analyze a Student Model

Read Nahee's opinion essay closely. The red side notes are the comments that her teacher, Mr. Plausky, wrote.

Nahee Chung

November 9

Libraries Teach Us How to Think

School libraries hold tons of information we'll never look at more than once, and even more information we'll never even see. So why are school libraries important? The other day I asked my father that question. "To learn how to think," he said.

Where is your opinion? Is it the same as your dad's?

I talked to our librarian, Ms. Walker. She said that my dad was on the right track. She told me that the library teaches students the science of information, which is basically two things: how to find information, and how to figure out if the information we find is good.

Excellent use of first-hand information.

I pointed to the encyclopedias across the room and said that no one I knew used an encyclopedia. Most kids get their information online. Ms. Walker took me downstairs and showed me six computers and four tablets. She told me that the library started loaning eBooks to fourth- and fifth-graders at the beginning of last year. I asked her how many eBooks the library has. She told me

You present both sides of the opinion here.

that the school has bought 380 eBooks, and there are about 210 fourth- and fifth-graders in our school. That is a pretty good number of eBook titles per student. Most elementary schools have less than one eBook title per student. Some don't have eBooks at all.

I like how you use the data from your sources.

Ms. Walker asked me, "How do you know if the information you find online is true or if it's made up?" I told her that I wasn't sure. She told me to come see her the next time I had a topic to research. She promised to show me where all of the good, reliable information is. Knowing the information I am using for schoolwork is accurate will be a relief!

Good use of direct quotes. Makes me feel like I was there.

So, now I know why school libraries are important. Unlike square roots or the main export of Venezuela, we'll remember to use what we learn there. We need libraries to help us learn more about the world, and, consequently, how to think about it.

I like how you conclude with your opinion, but it should be stated clearly.

Discuss and Decide

Does Nahee convince you that schools need libraries? If so, cite evidence from her essay that makes you think so. If she doesn't convince you, why not?

Be Clear!

When you write, always check your work. Did you write what you meant to say? In her essay, Nahee could have stated some of her ideas more clearly.

Here is a confusing sentence from Nahee's essay:

Unlike square roots or the main export of Venezuela, we'll remember to use what we learn there.

How could Nahee make her ideas more clear? She could state them in a more simple way. Here's an example:

They hold accurate information that we will use in the future.

Essay Tips

Remember These Tips When Writing!

- Read a sentence out loud if you are not sure it sounds right. Would your teacher write it the way you wrote it?
- Have a friend look at what you wrote. Does your friend understand what you mean?

Look back through Nahee's essay. Find one sentence that you could improve and underline it. Then rewrite the sentence so that it is more clear. Exchange your work with a partner. Ask your partner if what you wrote is easier to understand than what Nahee wrote.

Step 2 Practice the Task

Is art class important?

You will read:

- **An Editorial**
  Our Children Need Math, Above All Else
- **A Blog**
  Why I Love Art
- **A Magazine Article**
  Turning It Around

You will write:

- **An Opinion Essay**
  Is art class important?

Source 1: Editorial

AS YOU READ Analyze the editorial. Note information that helps you decide where you stand on the issue: Is art class important?

Our Children Need Math, Above All Else

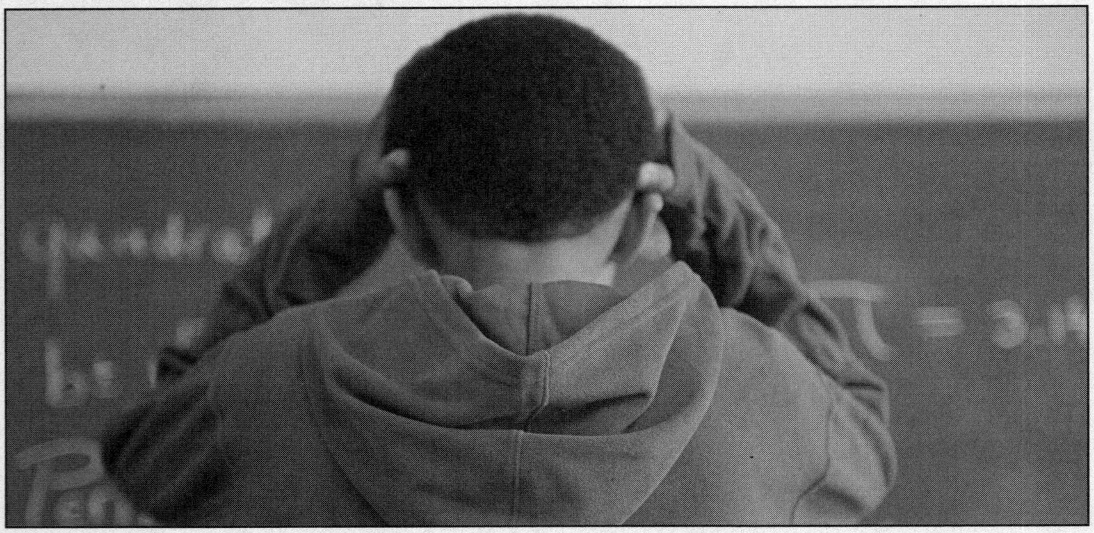

By Gonzalo Montoya

Here is some upsetting news: In the last decade, schools across the U.S. have revisited their teaching standards. You would think this would mean improved results in all subjects, right? Well, you'd be wrong. The U.S. falls behind other countries in critical math skills. In 2011, the United States ranked eleventh out of fifty-seven international school systems in fourth-grade math. We ranked ninth out of fifty-six international school systems in eighth-grade math. According to data published by the National Center for Education Statistics, the

U.S. is only 8% above the fourth-grade international achievement average, and 1.8% above the eighth-grade international achievement average.

Is this the type of math achievement our country should expect? If the future of our economy is tied to our children's ability to compete for work in the math, science, and technology sectors, I should say not. Math teaches students logical and critical thinking, which are important life skills to have.

Some people will argue that schools need to give students more time to explore their creativity in art classes. I disagree. Students can take art classes outside of school time. They can be creative when they play after school or on the weekends. Parents can take their children to see live performances or participate in other extracurricular activities. Art classes take time away from other subjects, including math. Students can do without art in their day-to-day lives, but they cannot do without math.

Schools need to do more with fewer resources, which is a difficult task. As I watch schools cut back on programs and staff in response to shrinking budgets, I am saddened and angered. But if schools do not focus what limited resources they do have on teaching math, I will be shocked.

We need to fight for math, above every other subject. Without math skills, our students will be lost.

Discuss and Decide

According to the author, what is one reason art classes should not be part of the school day?

Source 2: Blog

AS YOU READ Analyze the blog. Make notes that help you decide where you stand on the issue: Is art class important?

Home | About | Blog Life | Archive

Search This Website

Why I Love Art

A BLOG BY CHERISE

May 26

Here in the city, it's definitely springtime. My best inspiration comes at this time of year. Recently I've been in Central Park working on the collage pictured here.

ABOUT ME

Hi, I'm Cherise!

I am a fifth-grader who lives and goes to school in New York City. I love to make art, specifically collage. I started this blog to share some of my work. Hope you like it!

I love art. It's how I express myself best. It's not like other school subjects—there are no wrong answers! When I'm working creatively, the only decisions that count are the ones I make. I can experiment and take risks. And when I make a mistake, it's OK. As Samuel Beckett said, "No matter. Try again. Fail again. Fail better."

Some things can't be said. They can only be felt. Art makes me feel better about myself, my life, and all the problems of today's world.

So this spring, make sure you take an art class. Or visit a museum. Or maybe just go outside with a pencil and paper. You never know what may inspire you! Please share what projects you're working on in the comments!

COMMENTS

4 hours ago

Seven89

I'm working on blending pastels!

Sign me up! ♥ Enter your email address:

Discuss and Decide

According to the author, what makes art different from other school subjects?

Source 3: Magazine Article

AS YOU READ Analyze the magazine article. Make notes that help you decide where you stand on the issue: Is art class important?

Turning It Around

By Jabian Mendez

Batiste Cultural Arts Academy was once the lowest-performing school in Louisiana. Today, it is part of a program called Turnaround Arts. There are eight schools from across the United States in the program.

The Turnaround Arts program was created because of a study that showed that students who took art classes in schools began to develop better habits. One of these changes was increased class attendance. Another positive change was stronger performances in academics. Students who did art in school were also more likely to do extracurricular activities. This study also showed that students who do art in school are more likely to attend college and get a job.

Baptiste Cultural Arts Academy students take art and music classes. These subjects are taught near the end of school. This gives students a reason to look forward to being at school for an entire day. The Academy wants to help its students, and hopes to teach them to be leaders and thinkers by connecting them to the arts.

The students at Baptiste Cultural Arts Academy have benefited from their involvement with the arts. In one year, students improved by 29 points on state-issued performance tests. They experienced positive results in math performance levels. In the past, 21 percent of students were on track to go to college. Now, that number is up to 55 percent. It's pretty clear that having art in schools helps students improve academically.

Discuss and Decide

According to the article, what is one positive change that resulted from the Turnaround Arts program?

Respond to Questions

These questions will help you analyze the sources you read. Use your notes and refer to the sources in order to answer the questions. Your answers to these questions will help you write your essay.

1. Which source(s) agree that art class is important? How do you know? Make notes about reasons in the chart.

Source	Agrees that Art Class Is Important?	Reasons
Editorial Our Children Need Math, Above All Else	☐ yes ☐ no	
Blog Why I Love Art	☐ yes ☐ no	
Magazine Article Turning It Around	☐ yes ☐ no	

2 **Prose Constructed-Response** What is one reason why art class **is** important? Cite text evidence in your response.

3 **Prose Constructed-Response** What is one reason why art class **isn't** important? Cite text evidence in your response.

Planning and Prewriting

Before you draft your essay, complete some important planning steps.

Assignment

Write an opinion essay to answer the question: Is art class important?

What's Your Opinion?

Think about what you've read and respond below.

You may prefer to plan on a computer.

Issue: Is art class important?

Your position on the issue: ☐ yes ☐ no

Your opinion:

____

____

____

What Are Your Reasons?

Pick three sentences from the sources that helped you form your opinion. Write one sentence in each box below.

Reason	Reason	Reason

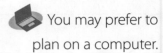

Finalize Your Plan

You know what your opinion is on the issue. Now, it's time to plan the structure of your essay. You will save time and create a more organized, logical essay by planning the structure before you start writing..

Use your responses on pages 18–20 to complete the graphic organizer.

Introduction

◀ Grab your reader's attention with an interesting fact or story. Identify the issue and your opinion.

Reason	Reason	Reason

◀ State reasons that support your opinion.

Opposing Opinion

◀ Give the opposing opinion and how you will counter it.

Concluding Section

◀ Restate your opinion.

Draft Your Essay

If you drafted your essay on the computer, you may wish to print it out.

As you write, think about:

- **Purpose** *what you want to communicate*
- **Clarity** *ideas that are straightforward and understandable*
- **Support** *examples from the sources that support your opinion*
- **Organization** *the logical structure for your essay*
- **Connecting Words** *words that link your ideas*
- **Academic Vocabulary** *words used in writing about a particular topic*

Revision Checklist: Self-Evaluation

Use the checklist below to guide your self-evaluation.

Ask Yourself	Make It Better
1. Does your introduction grab the audience's attention?	A great introduction hooks your audience. Ask a question, create a vivid image, or tell a personal story. Make sure you clearly state your opinion up front.
2. Do the reasons support your opinion?	In the body of your essay, give three reasons that support your opinion. Give details or examples to support these reasons.
3. Do connecting words help organize and link ideas in your essay?	Connecting words link ideas together. Use connecting words to signal differences of opinion, explain how two ideas relate, or shift from one paragraph of your essay to the next.
4. Does the essay explain and counter an opposing opinion?	Ask yourself, "What would someone who disagrees with my opinion say about my reasons?" Include an opposing viewpoint and explain how you counter it.
5. Does the last section restate your opinion?	In wrapping up your essay, restate your opinion and provide a summary of the reasons you gave to support your opinion.

Revision Checklist: Peer Review

Exchange your essay with a classmate, or read it out loud to your partner. As you read and comment on your partner's essay, focus on organization and evidence. You do not need to agree with your partner's opinion. Help your partner find parts of the draft that need to be revised.

What to Look For	Notes for My Partner
1. Does the introduction grab the audience's attention?	
2. Do the reasons support the stated opinion?	
3. Do connecting words help organize and link ideas in the essay?	
4. Does the essay explain and counter an opposing opinion?	
5. Does the last section restate the opinion?	

Use Connecting Words

Review Your Use of Connecting Words

To make your essay read smoothly and to link your ideas, use connecting words. Connecting words show how two things or ideas are related.

These sentences are choppy and interrupt the flow of ideas:

I love art for so many reasons. Mostly because it's how I express myself best.

This sentence is smooth and links both ideas together:

I love art because it's how I express myself best.

Essay Tips

Use Connecting Words!

Here are some connecting words that you might use when you revise your essay.

as a result	in contrast	rather
because	instead	specifically
consequently	nevertheless	therefore
despite	otherwise	unlike

Edit

Edit your essay to correct spelling, grammar, and punctuation errors.

Step 3 Perform the Task

How much homework should teachers assign?

You will read:

- **A Newspaper Editorial**
  Keep Schoolwork at School
- **A Letter To Parents**
  from Principal Reed
- **A Survey**
  How Much Time Do You Spend on Homework?

You will write:

- **An Opinion Essay**
  How much homework should teachers assign?

Source 1: School Newspaper Editorial

AS YOU READ
Look for reasons that support your opinion, or reasons that make you change your opinion about this question: How much homework should teachers assign?

Notes

The Wright School Weekly

Keep Schoolwork at School

By Audrey Dimola

I think homework does more harm than good. I'll share the reasons I feel this way. I also interviewed my teacher, Mrs. Duffy, about why she believes homework is helpful. Her opinions are in bold.

Homework makes up for lost time. Mrs. Duffy told me that the amount of time she is given to teach her students each day gets shorter every year. She says she gives homework to make sure we have enough time to learn. I think that students feel pressured because we have to make up for lost class time at home. How can more stress be good?

Homework supports what we learn at school. I learned from Mrs. Duffy that homework helps us to remember what we learn during the day. I say, if you listen in class, you'll remember what is taught. Should the whole class have to do extra work because of a few students who didn't pay attention?

Homework makes us successful. Mrs. Duffy says that research shows that students who complete their homework do better academically. But I think there are other reasons that students do well, too. Some students do well because they are close with family who can help them study, or they visit museums, or they do sports. Some students I know read for fun, and they say they learn more reading on their own than in school.

Homework makes us responsible. Mrs. Duffy tells me, "Learning to do what's expected of you is a good lesson to learn." I know that being responsible is a good thing, but some students have part-time jobs after school. Some of us babysit our brothers, sisters, or cousins. Many young people I know already have more responsibility than they can manage.

I think we should have the opportunity to complete all the work that's expected of us during school hours. That's why they call it "schoolwork," right? What are your thoughts? Send your opinions to The Wright School Weekly at wrightschoolpaper@wright.com.

Close Read

What does Audrey say to counter the argument that homework makes kids responsible?

Notes

Source 2: Letter to Parents

AS YOU READ
Write down comments or questions in the side margins. Continue to note information that helps you form an opinion about this question: How much homework should teachers assign?

Notes

MacArthur
Regional School

From: Principal Reed
MacArthur Regional School

Re: Homework

Dear parents,

It has come to my attention that there is some concern about the amount of homework teachers are assigning in their classes. Homework is an important part of students' learning. I'd like to set your minds at ease regarding this issue.

Homework reinforces what students learn in the classroom. The more students practice, the better they will become in each subject. They may learn how to solve a math problem or construct a sentence, but they may not have enough time to practice it in class. Homework is designed to be an added practice.

Homework gives students the opportunity to discover what they don't understand. A lesson might have made sense in class, but when students do the assignment at home, they might realize that something wasn't clear to them. They can discuss any problems with their teacher the next day to improve their understanding.

Notes

Students are better prepared for tests when they complete homework assignments. They become comfortable with working out assignments on their own. They will need to develop the skill of working on their own because that is required for test-taking. Doing work at home will also help them with their time-management skills, which are also important when taking tests.

The teachers here at MacArthur Regional aim to assign no more than 60 minutes of homework a night. If your student is spending more than 60 minutes on homework, please contact myself or the teachers. We want to help your students get the best education possible. Homework should not be a punishment, but a way to help our students get the most out of their education.

Sincerely,

Principal Michael Reed

Close Read

What is one reason why Principal Reed supports assigning homework?

Source 3: Survey

How Much Time Do You Spend on Homework?

Recent data from the National Assessment of Educational Progress reveals that the amount of homework that 13- and 17-year-olds do each night has not changed much since 1984. Interestingly, it is today's 9-year-olds who have more homework than they did in the past.

The charts below show that the number of students with no homework has declined by 13% since the mid-eighties. That decline is matched by an increase in the percentage of students who spend less than an hour doing homework each night.

How Much Homework Did Nine-Year-Olds Have in 1984?

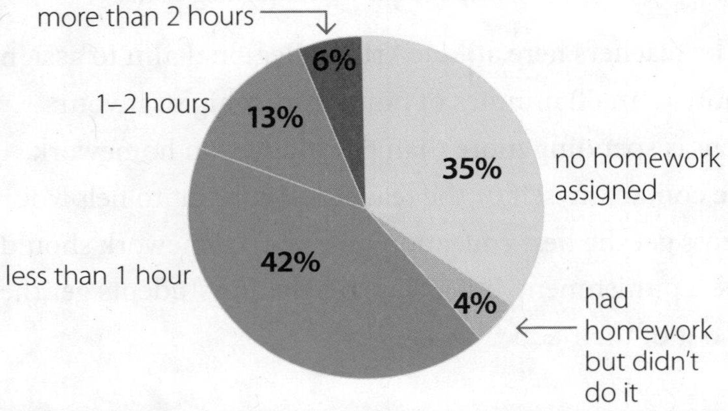

How Much Homework Did Nine-Year-Olds Have in 2012?

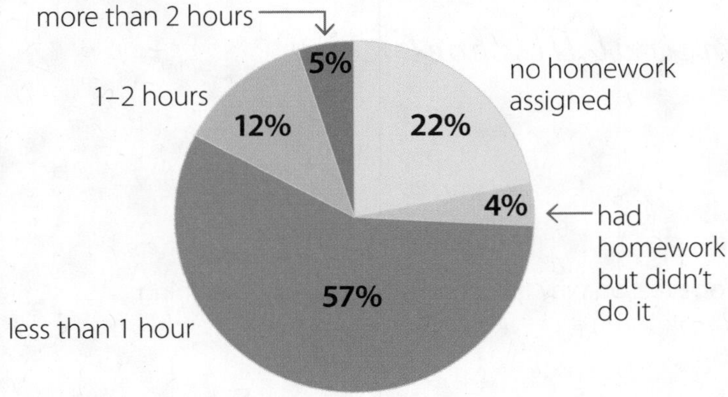

Discuss and Decide

Why has the percentage of students who have less than an hour of homework increased since 1984?

Respond to Questions

These questions will help you think about the sources you've read. Use your notes and refer to the sources to answer the questions. Your answers to these questions will help you write your essay.

1. According to Source 3, which of the following statements is true of nine-year-olds and homework in 2012?
   a. 8% of students had homework but didn't do it.
   b. 13% of students had 1–2 hours of homework.
   c. 25% of students did not have homework assigned to them.
   d. 57% of students had less than one hour of homework.

2. According to Source 1, why is homework difficult for some students?
   a. It helps students remember what they learned during the day.
   b. Students read more for fun than for school.
   c. Students might have other responsibilities at home, such as babysitting.
   d. Some students have a hard time listening in class.

3. Which words best support your answer to Question 2?
   a. "I learned from Mrs. Duffy that homework helps us to remember what we learn during the day." (lines 12–13)
   b. "Mrs. Duffy says that research shows that students who complete their homework do better academically." (lines 18–20)
   c. "Some students I know read for fun, and they say they learn more reading on their own than in school." (lines 23–25)
   d. "Many young people I know already have more responsibility than they can manage." (lines 30–32)

4 Which statement best supports the opinion that students should be given homework?

a. "Mrs. Duffy told me that the amount of time she is given to teach her students each day gets shorter every year." (Source 1)

b. "The more students practice, the better they will become in each subject." (Source 2)

c. "If your student is spending more than 60 minutes on homework, please contact myself or the teachers." (Source 2)

d. "That decline is matched by an increase in the percentage of students who spend less than an hour doing homework each night." (Source 3)

5 Which source(s) agree that students should have homework? How do you know? Record your reasons in the chart.

Source	Agrees that There Should Be Homework?	Reasons
Newspaper Editorial from Audrey Dimola	☐ yes ☐ no	
Letter to Parents from Principal Reed	☐ yes ☐ no	
Survey How Much Time Do You Spend on Homework?	☐ yes ☐ no	

6 **Prose-Constructed Response** In Source 1, how does Audrey organize her opinion? Cite evidence from the text in your response.

___

___

___

Write the Essay

Read the assignment.

Assignment

You have read about students and homework. Now write an opinion essay explaining how much homework teachers should assign students. Support your opinion with details from what you have read.

Plan

Use the graphic organizer to help you outline the structure of your opinion essay.

Introduction

◀ Grab your reader's attention with an interesting fact or story. Identify the issue and your opinion.

Reason | **Reason** | **Reason**

◀ State reasons that support your opinion.

Opposing Opinion

◀ Give the opposing opinion and how you will counter it.

Concluding Section

◀ Restate your opinion.

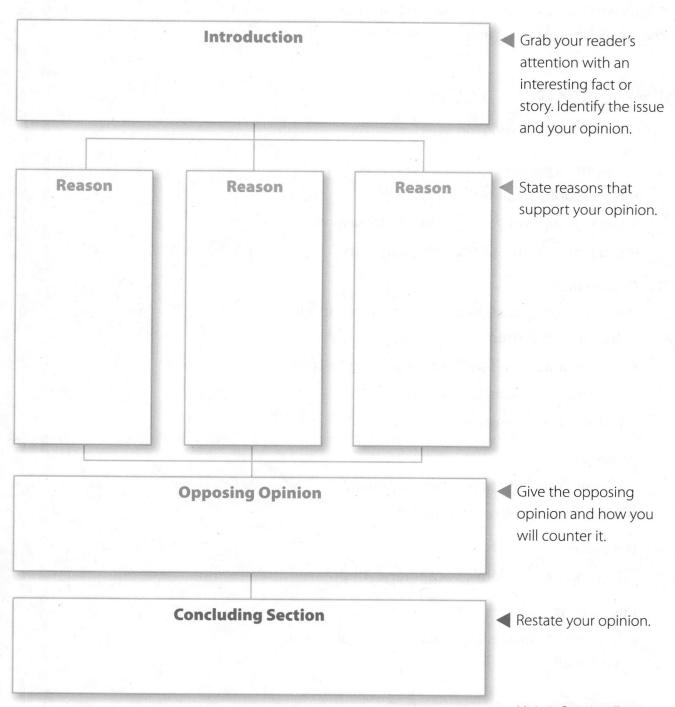

Draft

Use your notes and completed graphic organizer to write a first draft of your opinion essay.

Revise and Edit

Look back over your essay and compare it to the Evaluation Criteria. Revise your essay and edit it to correct spelling, grammar, and punctuation errors.

You may wish to draft and edit your essay on the computer.

Evaluation Criteria

Your teacher will be looking for:

1. ***Statement of purpose***
   - Is your opinion stated clearly?
   - Did you support your opinion with reasons?
   - Did you mention an opposing opinion?
2. ***Organization***
   - Are the sections of your essay organized in a way that makes sense?
   - Is there a smooth flow from beginning to end?
   - Did you use connecting words?
   - Is there a clear conclusion?
3. ***Reasons***
   - Do your reasons support your opinion?
   - Are your reasons convincing?
4. ***Vocabulary***
   - Did you use academic vocabulary?
5. ***Conventions***
   - Did you use proper punctuation, capitalization, and spelling?

Early American Heroes

Unit 2

Informative Essay

Step 1 **Analyze the Model**

Evaluate an informative essay about events in the life of the unusual hero Ann Bailey.

Step 2 **Practice the Task**

Write an informative essay about the events that led to Tecumseh's fight with the settlers.

Step 3 **Perform the Task**

Write an informative essay comparing the experiences of the explorer York during and after his expedition.

An informative essay is a short piece of nonfiction writing that presents facts about a topic. Its purpose is to provide accurate information to the reader. Informative essays are usually about actual people, events, or places. Examples of informative writing include articles in encyclopedias, newspapers, and magazines, as well as biographies and speeches.

The sources in this unit present factual information about three amazing figures from American history.

IN THIS UNIT, you will evaluate the way writers organized their informative essays, and analyze information from nonfiction articles, journal entries, a map, a timeline, and a speech. Then you will use what you have learned to write an informative essay of your own.

Step 1 **Analyze the Model**

What made Ann Bailey a hero?

You will read:

- **A Magazine Article**
  Mad Ann Bailey
- **A Sidebar to an Article**
  The Howl upon the Helm

You will analyze:

- **A Student Model**
  Courageous and Outrageous

Source 1: Magazine Article

The following text was used by Mr. McLaren's student, Dolores Vegas, as one of her sources for an essay answering the question "What made Ann Bailey a hero?" As you read, make notes in the side columns. Underline information that you find helpful.

Notes

Mad Ann Bailey

In 1761, Ann Hennis left her home in Liverpool, England, and moved to America. She was 19 years old, poor, and had lost both of her parents. She settled in Virginia and married Richard Trotter, a settler.

The number of settlers moving inland kept increasing, and so did the trouble between them and the American Indians living there. Virginia's governor organized local militias to join the fight, which ended in a victory for the settlers at the Battle of Point Pleasant. The costs were high, and among the militia's dead was Richard Trotter.

Ann's response to her husband's death was extreme. She learned how to use a gun—and a tomahawk—and became a frontier scout and messenger, riding hundreds of miles delivering messages between forts. She dressed in men's clothing, which allowed her to ride and fight, as women's clothing of the time would have got in her way.

Notes

She continually urged men to join the militia and to aid in the fight against the American Indians, and often warned settlers of looming attacks. Her abilities earned her great respect, and her eccentric ways earned her the name "Mad Ann." Ann married John Bailey, another scout, and together they moved to a settlement that was also the home of Fort Lee. (This is now the site of the present-day city of Charleston, West Virginia.)

In 1791, Fort Lee was under siege from American Indian warriors. The defenders were running low on gunpowder, and a request was made for a volunteer to ride 100 miles to Fort Union and return with fresh powder. All of the men in the militia remained silent, but Mad Ann volunteered. She rode without stopping across the wilderness, crossing rivers and streams, finally reaching Fort Union. Another horse was provided, loaded with the gunpowder the settlers at Fort Lee needed. Ann refused to have an escort for her return trip, thinking that it would slow her down. She made it back safely on the third day after she had left the besieged fort. Mad Ann had saved the settlement.

Notes

In addition to the known details of Ann's life, there are many remarkable stories about her that can't be proved or disproved. It is said that she was once chased by a band of Shawnee Indians, and hid in a log. The Shawnee couldn't discover Ann's hiding place, even though they rested on the same log. They took her horse, but during the night Ann snuck into their camp and took it back. She rode for a distance, and then began screaming wildly. From that moment on, the Shawnee believed her to be possessed and did not bother her. This would have been very helpful to her, because after John Bailey's death, Ann apparently lived outdoors, mostly in a cave, for more than ten years. She made her last deliveries as a messenger at the age of 75, but she lived for another eight years.

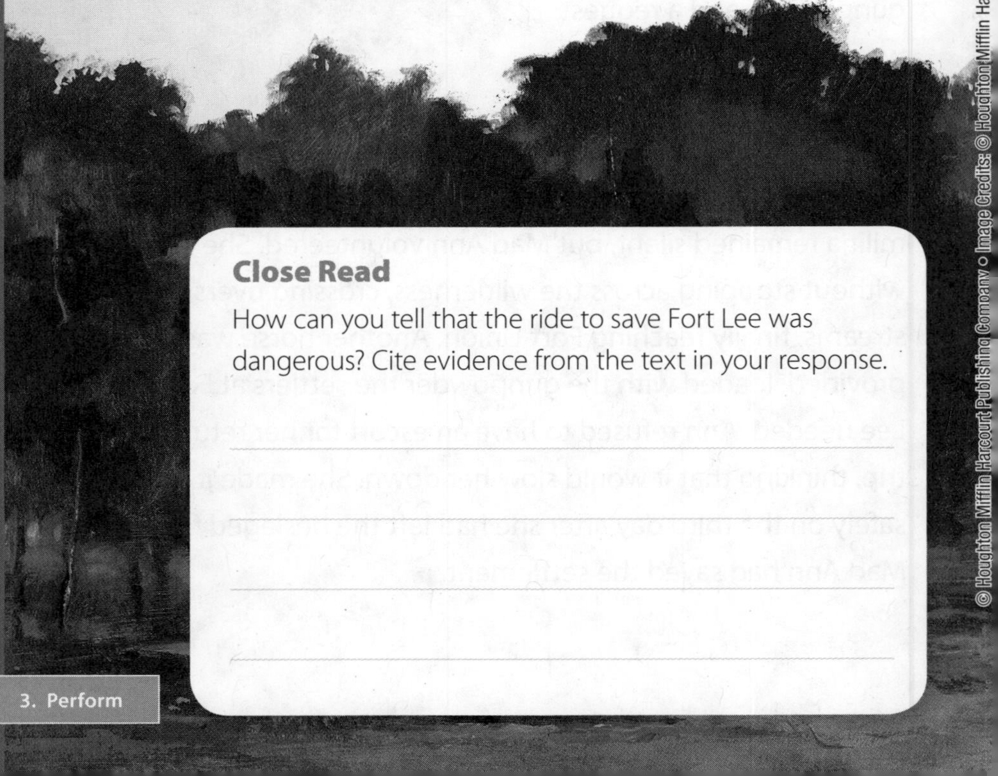

Close Read

How can you tell that the ride to save Fort Lee was dangerous? Cite evidence from the text in your response.

Source 2: Sidebar to a Magazine Article

Dolores used this sidebar as a second source for her essay. Continue to make notes in the side columns as you read. Underline information that you find helpful.

The Howl upon the Helm

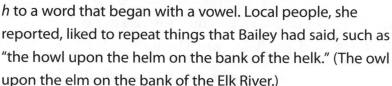

In 1823, Anne Royall, regarded as America's first woman travel writer, interviewed Ann Bailey. Royall noted Bailey's dialect, in which she added an *h* to a word that began with a vowel. Local people, she reported, liked to repeat things that Bailey had said, such as "the howl upon the helm on the bank of the helk." (The owl upon the elm on the bank of the Elk River.)

Royall questioned Bailey about her daring ride, and asked if she had been afraid. "I knew I could only be killed once, and I had to die sometime," was the response. Bailey had made her way across the wilderness by following the traces left by Lewis's army. She had crossed rivers by fording, swimming, or making rafts. As she said, "I halways carried a hax . . . and I could chop has well has hany man."

When asked what the general had said when she returned to the fort with the needed gunpowder, Bailey said, "Why, you're a brave soldier, Ann."

Discuss and Decide

What was Ann Bailey's attitude toward danger? How did her attitude help her?

Notes

Analyze a Student Model

Dolores wrote an essay that answered the question: What made Ann Bailey a hero? The red notes are the comments that her teacher, Mr. McLaren, wrote.

Dolores Vegas

September 21

Courageous and Outrageous

Great title!

Heroes are not like everyone else. They do the unexpected, they take risks, and they surprise those around them. Mad Ann Bailey was a hero.

good opening paragraph

Bailey's behavior wasn't expected from a woman of the late 1700s. She challenged people's opinions, but she earned their respect through her daring escapades. Perhaps her husband's death made something snap in Bailey. Whatever it was, she seems to have suddenly become an eccentric, larger-than-life character. She devoted herself to her mission to help and defend settlers, people who were like her late husband.

I like this background information.

To some, Bailey may have seemed crazed, but it could just as easily have been determination. Perhaps there was also a bit of revenge there, we don't know. Living

The way you've organized this essay really works.

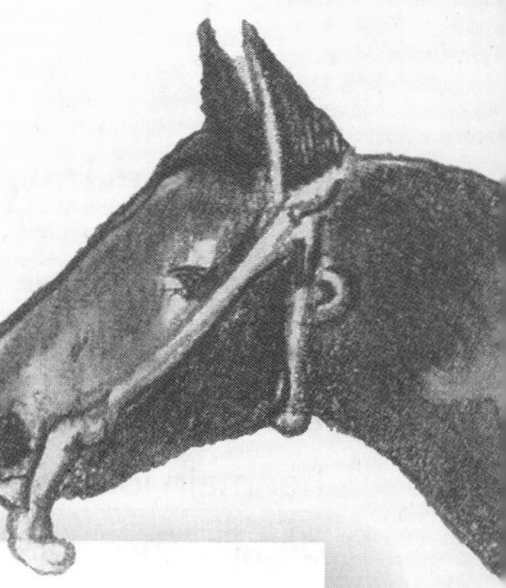

her life as a scout and messenger in those dangerous times made Bailey a hero, but volunteering when no man would makes her an even bigger hero.

When Bailey explained her courage to Anne Royall, she said "I had to die sometime." It's clear that Bailey was made of some powerful stuff. Was it in her all along, waiting to be triggered? Or did her husband's death bring about the character of Mad Ann?

Interesting points. Is there a better word for "stuff"?

Discuss and Decide

According to Dolores, what made Ann Bailey a hero?

Organizing an Informative Essay

You can organize the facts in an informative essay in various ways. In the student model, "Courageous and Outrageous," Dolores used main idea and details. In her first paragraph, Dolores stated her main idea. The following paragraphs supply supporting details. The final paragraph neatly wraps up the essay.

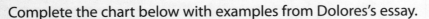

Complete the chart below with examples from Dolores's essay.

Introduction

◀ The first paragraph introduces the main idea of the essay. It often includes an interesting detail, question, or idea.

Detail

◀ The following paragraphs support the main idea with details and examples.

Detail

Detail

Conclusion

◀ The final paragraph often restates the main idea, and includes a further insight or observation.

Step 2 Practice the Task

What led Tecumseh to fight?

You will read:

- **A Historical Timeline**
  Tecumseh's Life
- **An Informational Article**
  The Battle of Point Pleasant
- **A Speech**
  Tecumseh's Address to General William Henry Harrison, 1810

You will write:

- **An Informative Essay**
  What led Tecumseh to fight?

Source 1: Historical Timeline

AS YOU READ You will be writing an essay that explores what led Tecumseh to fight. Identify people and events that made an impact on Tecumseh. These notes will help you write your essay.

Tecumseh's Life

As the United States expanded during the late 1700s, white settlers moved farther and farther west. When they encountered American Indian communities, there were often fights as the settlers tried to claim the land. Tecumseh was born into this conflict and grew up to be one of the most important American Indian leaders of his time.

1768
Tecumseh is born to the Shawnee tribe near what is now Springfield, Ohio.

1774
Tecumseh's father is killed at the Battle of Point Pleasant. His mother later moves to Missouri with other Shawnee.

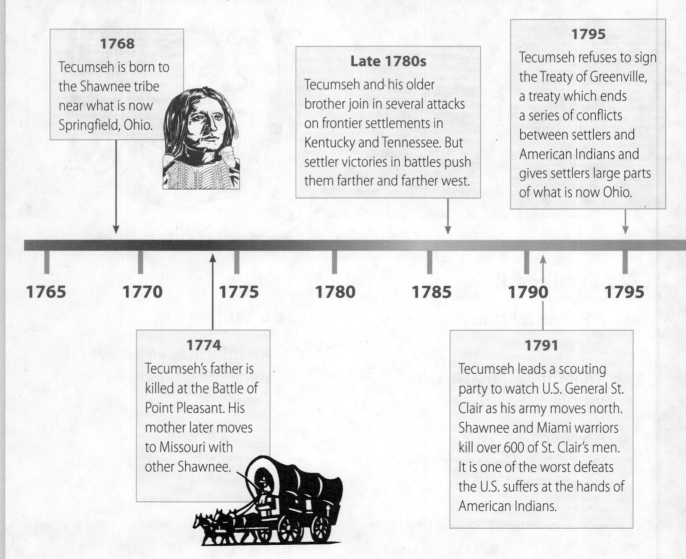

Late 1780s
Tecumseh and his older brother join in several attacks on frontier settlements in Kentucky and Tennessee. But settler victories in battles push them farther and farther west.

1791
Tecumseh leads a scouting party to watch U.S. General St. Clair as his army moves north. Shawnee and Miami warriors kill over 600 of St. Clair's men. It is one of the worst defeats the U.S. suffers at the hands of American Indians.

1795
Tecumseh refuses to sign the Treaty of Greenville, a treaty which ends a series of conflicts between settlers and American Indians and gives settlers large parts of what is now Ohio.

1765 | 1770 | 1775 | 1780 | 1785 | 1790 | 1795

1805
Tecumseh's brother, Tenskwatawa, becomes a respected spiritual leader. He preaches about returning to a traditional way of life for the Shawnee. Tecumseh will believe his teachings after he predicts the solar eclipse of 1806.

1808
Tecumseh and his brother establish a village at Prophetstown, located in Indiana. Many people from various tribes gather here.

1809
Tecumseh begins to travel through the Midwest and the South. He urges different tribes, even longtime enemies, to form a confederacy to resist losing any more land to settlers.

1810
Tecumseh organizes the Ohio Valley Confederacy, which includes people from the Shawnee, Potawatomi, Kickapoo, Winnebago, Menominee, Ottawa, and Wyandot nations.

1811
The Battle of Tippecanoe. While Tecumseh is traveling, U.S. troops led by William Henry Harrison attack Tenskwatawa in Prophetstown. Tenskwatawa is defeated and the village is burned to the ground.

1812
Tecumseh makes an alliance with the British during the War of 1812 to stop the U.S. from expanding further west. The alliance scores several victories against the U.S.

1813
Tecumseh clashes with William Henry Harrison at the Battle of the Thames. Tecumseh is killed, and his alliance of American Indian nations dies with him.

1800 1805 1810 1815

Discuss and Decide

How did Tecumseh resist attempts by people who were not native to settle on American Indian land? Cite text evidence in your response.

Source 2: Informational Article

AS YOU READ Analyze the article. Continue to write notes and underline information that will help you write your essay.

The Battle of Point Pleasant

by Barry deWitt

In 1774, fighting increased between Shawnee Indians and settlers in the Ohio Valley (what is now West Virginia) as the settlers moved farther west into American Indian land. Lord Dunmore, the governor of the colony of Virginia, decided to attack the Shawnee to stop their resistance. He formed two armies—one in the north that he led himself, and one in the south led by Andrew Lewis. The Shawnee chief Cornstalk knew they were coming and decided to attack Lewis's southern army before it could meet up with Dunmore's northern army.

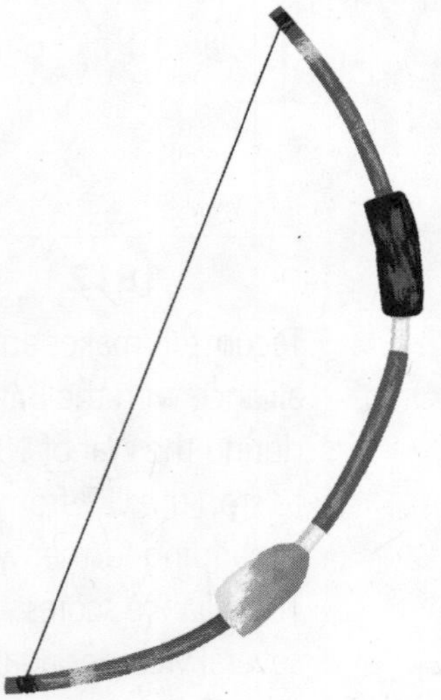

On October 10, Cornstalk's warriors crossed the Ohio River under the cover of night. They hoped they could catch Lewis's troops sleeping, but some were awake already and let the others know. Both sides started the battle with about one thousand men. Fog filled the battleground that morning, and with the smoke from all the guns firing, it was hard to see. Most of the fighting was up close and hand-to-hand. The conflict, now called the Battle of Point Pleasant, was confusing, bloody, and intense. It lasted until the late afternoon and many men died on both sides. Eventually the Shawnee retreated, and the Virginians won the battle.

Peace came to the Ohio Valley, but only for a short time. One of the warriors who died at the Battle of Point Pleasant was Pucksinwah, a Shawnee chief and the father of Tecumseh. With his dying breath, he told his oldest son to train the young Tecumseh to be a warrior and to never make peace with the settlers.

Close Read

Why would Pucksinwah want Tecumseh to become a warrior? Cite text evidence in your response.

Source 3: Speech

AS YOU READ Analyze the speech. Continue to underline and circle information that you may cite as textual evidence when you write your essay.

Excerpt from

Tecumseh's Address to General William Henry Harrison, 1810

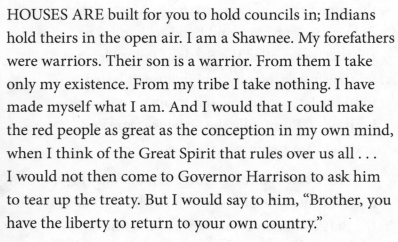

HOUSES ARE built for you to hold councils in; Indians hold theirs in the open air. I am a Shawnee. My forefathers were warriors. Their son is a warrior. From them I take only my existence. From my tribe I take nothing. I have made myself what I am. And I would that I could make the red people as great as the conception in my own mind, when I think of the Great Spirit that rules over us all . . . I would not then come to Governor Harrison to ask him to tear up the treaty. But I would say to him, "Brother, you have the liberty to return to your own country."

You wish to prevent the Indians from doing as we wish them, to unite and let them consider their lands as the common property of the whole. You take the tribes aside and advise them not to come into this measure . . . You want by your distinctions of Indian tribes, in allotting to each a particular, to make them war with each other. You never see an Indian endeavor to make the white people do this. You are continually driving the red people, when at last you will drive them onto the great lake, where they can neither stand nor work.

Since my residence at Tippecanoe, we have endeavored to level all distinction, to destroy village chiefs, by whom all mischiefs are done. It is they who sell the land to the Americans. Brother, this land that was sold, and the goods that were given for it, was only done by a few . . . In the future we are prepared to punish those who propose to sell land to the Americans. If you continue to purchase them, it will make war among the different tribes, and, at last I do not know what will be the consequences among the white people. Brother, I wish you would take pity on the red people and do as I have requested. If you will not give up the land and do cross the boundary of our present settlement, it will be very hard, and produce a great trouble between us.

The way, the only way to stop this evil is for the red men to unite in claiming a common and equal right in the land, as it was at first, and should be now—for it was never divided, but belongs to all. No tribe has the right to sell, even to each other, much less to strangers . . . Sell a country! Why not sell the air, the great sea, as well as the earth? Did not the Great Spirit make them all for the use of his children?

Discuss and Decide

What were Tecumseh's views on owning land, and how did they differ from those of the United States government?

Respond to Questions

These questions will help you examine the sources you read. Use your notes and refer to the sources in order to answer the questions. Your answers to these questions will help you write your essay.

1. Why did Tecumseh travel throughout the Midwest and the South asking different tribes to join him?
   - **a.** He wanted to attack General St. Clair.
   - **b.** He wanted tribes to unite to stop settlers from taking more Indian land away.
   - **c.** He wanted to return to a traditional Shawnee way of life.
   - **d.** He wanted to make an alliance with the British.

2. Which statements from Source 3 best describe the way Tecumseh felt about owning land?
   - **a.** "I am a Shawnee. My forefathers were warriors. Their son is a warrior."
   - **b.** "Houses are built for you to hold councils in; Indians hold theirs in the open air."
   - **c.** "You wish to prevent the Indians from doing as we wish them, to unite and let them consider their lands as the common property of the whole."
   - **d.** "You are continually driving the red people, when at last you will drive them onto the great lake, where they can neither stand nor work."

3. What is the best meaning of *confederacy* as it is used in "Tecumseh's Life"?
   - **a.** American Indians
   - **b.** tribe
   - **c.** settlers
   - **d.** alliance

4. Which of the following is a claim about Tecumseh you could make after reading the sources?

   a. Tecumseh's defeat at the Battle of Tippecanoe ended his hopes for an alliance of Indian nations.

   b. He followed his father's request to make peace with the settlers.

   c. He believed that the Shawnee were the only American Indians who could sell their land.

   d. He thought that an alliance of Indian nations was an important way of stopping the U.S. from taking Indian land.

5. **Prose Constructed-Response** Why did Tecumseh make an alliance with the British during the War of 1812? Cite text evidence from "Tecumseh's Life" in your response.

____

____

____

____

____

6. **Prose Constructed-Response** What are two reasons why Tecumseh chose to fight against the U.S. settlers? Cite text evidence in your response.

____

____

____

____

____

Planning and Prewriting

> **Assignment**
> Write an informative essay to answer the question: What led Tecumseh to fight?

When writing an informative essay, the first step is to think about its organization. The assignment asks you to think about what leads someone to do something. This is a clue that you could write a cause-and-effect essay, because cause-and-effect writing explains why something happens.

You may prefer to plan on a computer.

Collect Information

When you use information from a source, only include the material that applies to your topic. Don't include unnecessary information—it takes a reader's interest away from your main points.

Complete the chart to show what you'll use from each source.

Source	Evidence from Source	Cause and Effect
A Historical Timeline Tecumseh's Life		
An Informational Article The Battle of Point Pleasant		
A Speech Tecumseh's Address to General William Henry Harrison		

Finalize Your Plan

Use your responses and notes from previous pages to make a plan for your essay.

Introduction

◀ The first paragraph presents an overall look at the main causes and effects in the essay. It also often incudes an interesting quotation, question, or idea.

Cause and Effect

◀ The following paragraphs provide details that explain and support the ideas in your introduction.

Cause and Effect

Cause and Effect

Conclusion

◀ The final paragraph often restates the main idea, and has a further insight or observation.

Draft Your Essay

If you drafted your essay on the computer, you may wish to print it out.

As you write, think about:

- **Purpose** *to use sources to write a cause-and-effect essay*
- **Audience** *your teacher and your classmates*
- **Clarity** *easily understood relationships between causes and effects*
- **Support** *examples from the sources that support your main idea*
- **Organization** *the logical structure for your essay*
- **Connecting Words** *words that link your ideas*

Revision Checklist: Self-Evaluation

Use the checklist below to guide your self-evaluation.

Ask Yourself	Revision Strategies
1. Does the introduction present your main idea and hook the audience?	Clearly state your main idea. Try to include the most interesting fact from your sources in the first paragraph, or use a thought-provoking question or quotation.
2. Is the relationship between each cause and effect clear?	Make sure that each cause and its effect are clearly linked.
3. Does your essay flow well and connect the details to the main idea?	Read your words to see if they seem disconnected or jarring. Use connecting words and make ideas follow each other naturally.
4. Does the conclusion restate your main idea and leave a lasting impression on your reader?	Restate your main idea. Include an insight about the topic such as a question that will make the reader think more deeply about the topic.

Revision Checklist: Peer Review

Exchange your essay with a classmate. Read and comment on your partner's essay, focusing on how well it explains why Tecumseh chose to fight against the settlers.

Help your partner find parts of the draft that could be improved.

What to Look For	Notes for My Partner
1. Does the introduction present the main idea and hook the audience?	
2. Is the relationship between each cause and effect clear?	
3. Does the essay flow well and connect the details to the main idea?	
4. Does the conclusion restate the main idea and leave a lasting impression on the reader?	

Revision: Writing an Introduction

The best way to make readers interested in your work is to write a great introduction. One way to grab a reader's attention is to include a thought-provoking quote in your first paragraph. Make sure the quote is related to your main idea.

This introduction gets the reader's attention with an interesting quotation and states the point of the essay:

> "Sell a country! Why not sell the air, the great sea, as well as the earth? Did not the Great Spirit make them all for the use of his children?" This is how Tecumseh protested against the U.S. buying land that belonged to Indian tribes. He spent his whole life fighting against the U.S. settlers as they took Indian land again and again.

Essay Tips

Attention-Getting Advice

- Write a statement that makes the reader curious about the topic.
- Use an interesting, thought-provoking quote.
- Present a fact that will shock or surprise the reader.
- Write a brief account of a fascinating event.
- Ask a question that the reader can relate to.

Edit

Edit your essay to correct spelling, grammar, and punctuation errors.

Step 3 **Perform the Task**

How did York's life change after his adventure?

You will read:

- **An Informational Article**
  The Lewis and Clark Expedition, May 1804–September 1806
- **Journal Excerpts**
  Excerpts from Clark's Expedition Journals
- **An Informational Article**
  After the Expedition

You will write:

- **An Informative Essay**
  How did York's life change after his adventure?

Source 1: Informational Article

AS YOU READ
You will be writing a compare-and-contrast informative essay that explains how an explorer's life changed. As you read the sources, identify details that are similar, and ideas that differ. Underline and circle information that you may cite as textual evidence when you write your essay.

Notes

The Lewis and Clark Expedition

May 1804–September 1806

In 1804, nearly four-dozen men of the Corps of Discovery set off on a boat from St. Louis, Missouri. They were about to explore unknown U.S. territory west of the Mississippi River. More than two years later, the men

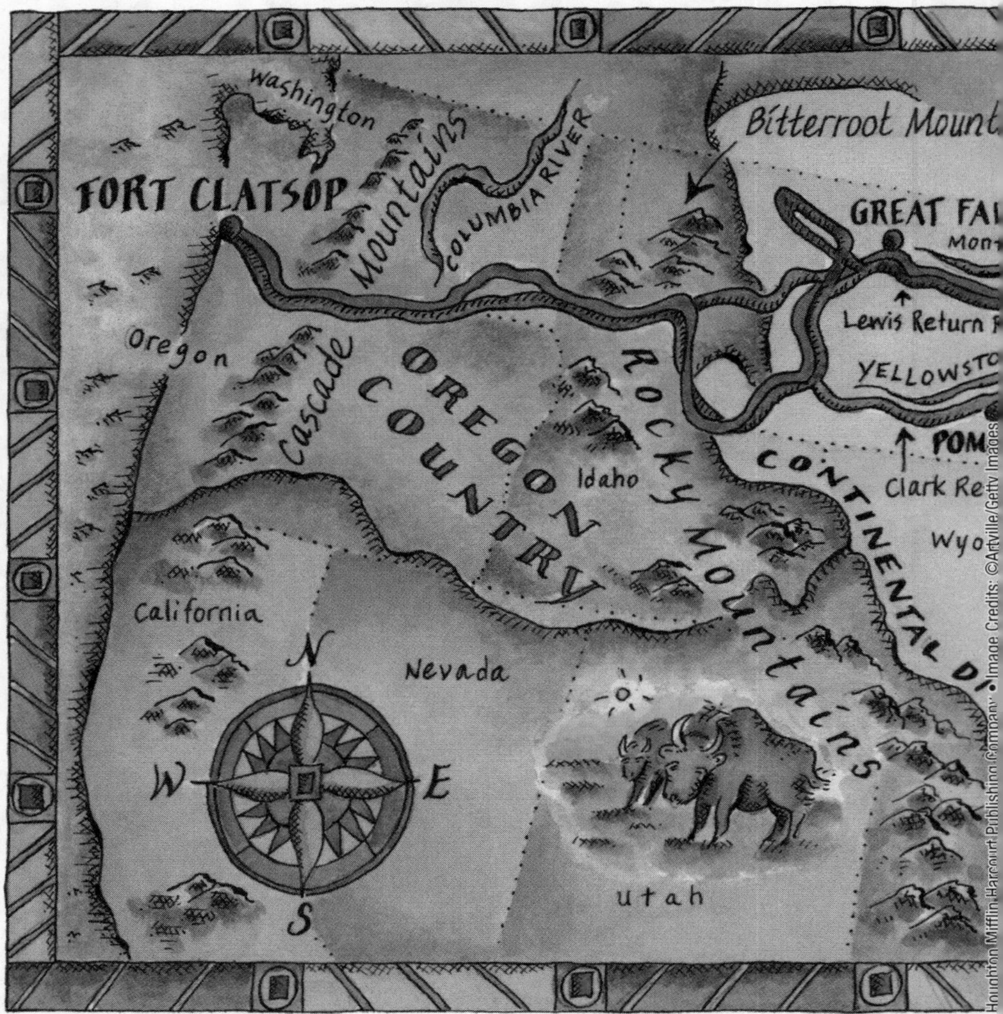

returned after an 8,000-mile journey. Led by Meriwether Lewis and William Clark, the members of the Corps of Discovery included a man named York. York had grown up as a companion to William Clark. However, Clark also kept York as a slave. Throughout the punishing journey, York held his own as an important part of the team that brought back information about the land, people, animals, and plants of the northwest.

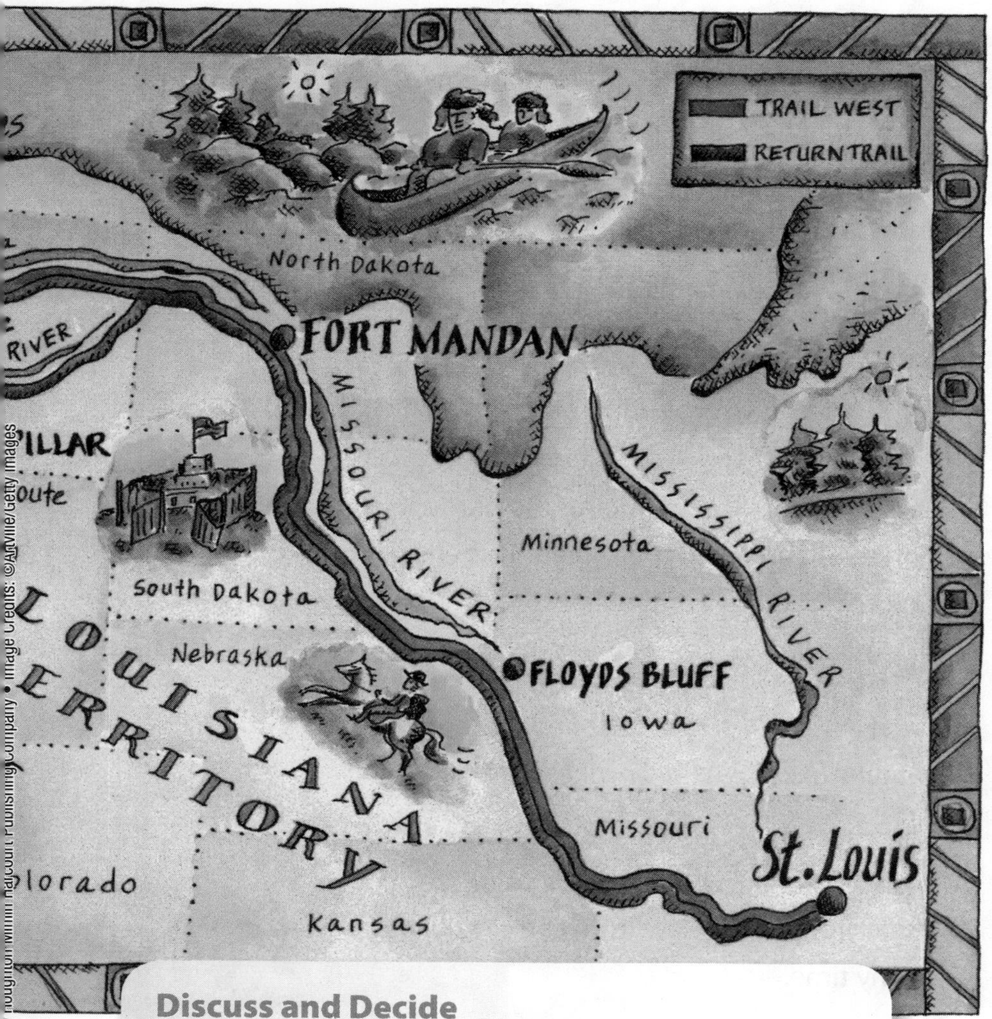

Notes

Discuss and Decide

What evidence from the text and map conveys the difficulty of Lewis and Clark's journey?

Source 2: Journal Excerpts

Notes

Excerpts from

Clark's Expedition Journals

edited by Frank Suzuki

The journals from the Lewis and Clark Expedition were nearly 5,000 pages long. Clark's journal is the source for several observations about his slave York.

June 5, 1804 *Here my servant York swam to the sand bar to gather greens for our dinner and returned with a sufficient quantity . . .*

It is clear that York helped gather food for the group, and it's likely that he also helped cook their meals. This entry shows that he could swim, which is something not all members of the group could do.

August 19, 1804 *Sgt. Floyd . . . is dangerously ill . . . I am much concerned for his situation. Every man is attentive to him (York principally).*

Sergeant Floyd, a member of the group, became very sick on the trip and eventually died. This entry is from the night before Floyd died, and tells of the care York gave to the sick man.

September 9, 1804 *I directed my servant York with me to kill a buffalo near the boat.*

York must have been well-trusted. He is obviously carrying a gun. Slaves were usually banned by law from carrying guns at any time.

November 18, 1805 *A little cloudy this morning. I set out with 10 men and my man York to the ocean by land.*

After reaching the northwest coast, the group journeyed to a beach to see the Pacific Ocean. York became the first African American to cross the United States.

December 28, 1805 *. . . York very unwell from violent colds and strains carrying in meat and lifting logs on the huts to build them.*

York got sick helping to build Fort Clatsop, where the group would spend the winter. In November, Clark had held a vote among the group to decide where to set up the camp. All members, including York, voted. York may have been the first African-American man to vote in the United States.

Close Read

How were York's experiences with the expedition unusual for a person who was held as a slave? Cite text evidence in your response.

Notes

Source 3: Informational Article

Notes

After the Expedition

by Gail Winters

The Corps of Discovery returned to St. Louis, Missouri, on September 23, 1806. They had only lost one man, Sergeant Floyd. The whole town of 1,000 people gathered on the riverbanks and greeted and congratulated the returning heroes. Even though people held as slaves were normally considered property, York received hearty congratulations, too. Not only had the Corps survived the incredible journey, but they had made geographic and scientific discoveries and mapped the land.

The members of the Corps of Discovery each received double pay and 320 acres of land—except for York. Even though Clark had named some small islands and a river after him, Clark refused to give York his freedom. York also had a wife who was owned by another master, and at first Clark wouldn't let him see her, and had York put in jail when he protested.

Clark finally freed York about ten years after they returned from the expedition. However, it isn't clear what happened to York after he became free. Many people believe that he started a freighting company between Kentucky and Tennessee, and that he died from cholera before 1832. Others have said that he went out west again to live with Native Americans in Wyoming.

Discuss and Decide

What are some ways in which York was treated differently from other members of the expedition?

Respond to Questions

The following questions will help you think about the sources you've read. Use your notes and refer to the sources as you answer the questions. Your answers will help you write the essay.

1. Which detail in Source 2 best describes York's treatment as an equal member of Lewis and Clark's group?
   - **a.** "A little cloudy this morning. I set out with 10 men and my man York to the ocean by land."
   - **b.** "Here my servant York swam to the sand bar to gather greens for our dinner . . ."
   - **c.** "Sgt. Floyd . . . is dangerously ill . . . I am much concerned for his situation."
   - **d.** "I directed my servant York with me to kill a buffalo near the boat."

2. Why did Clark put York in jail?
   - **a.** York protested when Clark wouldn't let him see his wife.
   - **b.** York was congratulated after returning to St. Louis.
   - **c.** York received extra money and land after returning to St. Louis.
   - **d.** York shot a buffalo with a gun during the journey west.

3. What is the best meaning for *expedition* as it is used in these sources?
   - **a.** camp
   - **b.** journey
   - **c.** journal
   - **d.** slave

4. Which of the following is a claim about York you could make after reading the sources?

   a. York had more freedom while traveling with Lewis and Clark's group than he did after returning to St. Louis in 1806.

   b. York had more freedom east of the Mississippi River than he did west of the Mississippi River.

   c. York was not a slave west of the Mississippi River.

   d. York did not do much for the Corps of Discovery.

5. **Prose Constructed-Response** How did York contribute to the Corps of Discovery during the journey? Cite details from Source 2 in your response.

6. **Prose Constructed-Response** Look at the map in Source 1 and the journal excerpts in Source 2. Which gives you a better understanding of York's experiences on the expedition? Cite text evidence in your response.

Write the Essay

Read the assignment.

Assignment

Write an informative essay answering the question: How did York's life change after his adventure? Compare and contrast York's experiences east and west of St. Louis. Cite text evidence from what you have read.

Plan

Use the graphic organizer to help you outline the structure of your informative essay.

Introduction

◀ Identify what you will be comparing and contrasting. State your main idea. Include an interesting detail, question, or quotation to hook your audience.

Key Point

Key Point

Key Point

◀ Compare and contrast one point about each subject at a time (point-by-point); or discuss all the points relating to the first subject before moving on to the second (subject-by-subject). Include relevant facts, concrete details, and other textual evidence to support your points.

Conclusion

◀ Summarize the key points and restate your main idea. Include an insight related to your main idea.

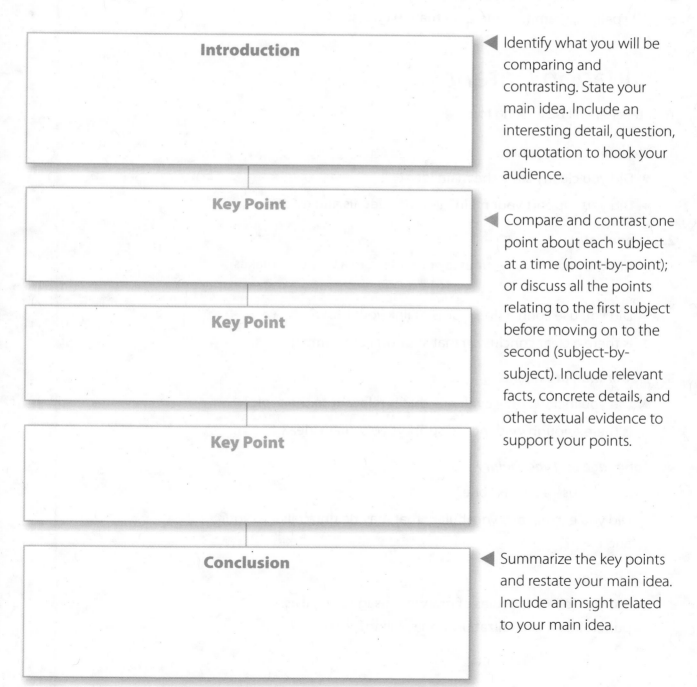

Draft

Use your notes and completed graphic organizer to write a first draft of your opinion essay.

Revise and Edit

Look back over your essay and compare it to the Evaluation Criteria. Revise your essay and edit it to correct spelling, grammar, and punctuation errors.

You may wish to draft and edit your essay on the computer.

Evaluation Criteria

Your teacher will be looking for:

1. ***Statement of purpose***
   - Did you clearly state the main idea?
   - Did you support your main idea with details and evidence?
2. ***Organization***
   - Are the sections of your essay organized in a way that makes sense?
   - Did you use connecting words to link your ideas?
   - Is there a clear conclusion that supports the comparisons?
3. ***Elaboration of evidence***
   - Did you include only evidence that is relevant to the topic?
   - Is there enough evidence to support your main idea?
4. ***Language and vocabulary***
   - Did you use a formal tone?
   - Did you explain any vocabulary that may be unfamiliar to your audience?
5. ***Conventions***
   - Did you follow the rules of grammar usage as well as punctuation, capitalization, and spelling?

The Way I See It

Unit 3

Response to Literature

Step 1

Analyze the Model

Evaluate a student model that analyzes how characters interact in a story.

Step 2

Practice the Task

Write a response to a short story explaining how a character's point of view influences how events are described.

Step 3

Perform the Task

Write a response to a short story explaining how the narrator can shape the way events are presented.

Lewis Carroll, the author of *Alice's Adventures in Wonderland* once said, "Literature adds to reality. It does not simply describe it." Think about what he means by this statement.

Some stories might take you to distant places or introduce you to people you might otherwise never meet. Others might make you think about familiar events in surprising ways. Keep Lewis Carroll's quote in mind as you read the stories in this unit. Consider what these stories add to reality.

IN THIS UNIT, you will evaluate a student's essay about how the characters at a very strange tea party interact. Then you will write a response to a story about the adventures of two puzzled ants. Finally, you will read a familiar story told from another point of view, and explain how the narrator presents the events in a different light.

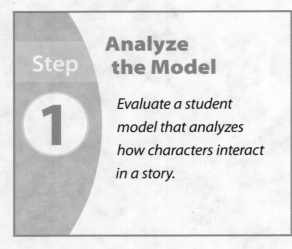

Step 1 **Analyze the Model**

How do characters interact in a story?

You will read:

- **An Excerpt from a Novel**
  "A Mad Tea-Party" from Alice's Adventures in Wonderland

You will analyze:

- **A Student Model**
  A Balancing Act

Source: Excerpt from a Novel

Ms. Jefferson's student, Guy Brown, used the following excerpt from *Alice's Adventures in Wonderland* as a source for an essay about how its characters interact. As you read, make notes in the side columns. Underline information that you find helpful.

Notes

A Mad Tea-Party

by Lewis Carroll

There was a table set out under a tree in front of the house, and the March Hare and the Hatter were having tea at it. A Dormouse was sitting between them, fast asleep, and the other two were using it as a cushion, resting their elbows on it, and talking over its head. "Very uncomfortable for the Dormouse," thought Alice; "only as it's asleep, I suppose it doesn't mind."

The table was a large one, but the three were all crowded together at one corner of it: "No room! No room!" they cried out when they saw Alice coming. "There's *plenty* of room!" said Alice indignantly, and she sat down in a large armchair at one end of the table.

"Have some punch," the March Hare said in an encouraging tone.

Alice looked all round the table, but there was nothing on it but tea. "I don't see any punch," she remarked.

"There isn't any," said the March Hare.

"Then it wasn't very civil of you to offer it," said Alice angrily.

"It wasn't very civil of you to sit down without being invited," said the March Hare.

"I didn't know it was *your* table," said Alice; "it's laid for a great many more than three."

"Your hair wants cutting," said the Hatter. He had been looking at Alice for some time with great curiosity, and this was his first speech.

"You should learn not to make personal remarks," Alice said with some severity; "it's very rude."

The Hatter opened his eyes very wide on hearing this; but all he *said* was "Why is a raven like a writing-desk?"

Discuss and Decide

Which actions tell you that the March Hare is argumentative?

Notes

Notes

Come, we shall have some fun now! thought Alice. *I'm glad they've begun asking riddles.* "I believe I can guess that," she added aloud.

"Do you mean that you think you can find out the answer to it?" said the March Hare.

"Exactly so," said Alice.

"Then you should say what you mean," the March Hare went on.

"I do," Alice hastily replied; "at least—at least I mean what I say—that's the same thing, you know."

"Not the same thing a bit!" said the Hatter. "Why, you might just as well say that 'I see what I eat' is the same thing as 'I eat what I see'!"

"You might just as well say," added the March Hare, "that 'I like what I get' is the same thing as 'I get what I like'!"

"You might just as well say," added the Dormouse, who seemed to be talking in his sleep, "that 'I breathe when I sleep' is the same thing as 'I sleep when I breathe'!"

"It *is* the same thing with you," said the Hatter; and here the conversation dropped, and the party sat silent for a minute, while Alice thought over all she could remember about ravens and writing-desks, which wasn't much.

"The Dormouse is asleep again," said the Hatter, and he poured a little hot tea upon its nose.

The Dormouse shook his head impatiently, and said, without opening his eyes, "Of course; just what I was going to remark myself."

"Have you guessed the riddle yet?" the Hatter said, turning to Alice again.

"No, I give it up," Alice replied: "what's the answer?"

"I haven't the slightest idea," said the Hatter.

"Nor I," said the March Hare.

Alice sighed wearily. "I think you might do something better with the time," she said, "than wasting it asking riddles that have no answers."

"Suppose we change the subject," the March Hare interrupted, yawning. "I'm getting tired of this. I vote the young lady tells us a story."

"I'm afraid I don't know one," said Alice, rather alarmed at the proposal.

"Then the Dormouse shall!" they both cried. "Wake up, Dormouse!" And they pinched it on both sides at once.

The Dormouse slowly opened his eyes. "I wasn't asleep," he said in a hoarse, feeble voice. "I heard every word you fellows were saying."

"Tell us a story!" said the March Hare.

"Yes, please do!" pleaded Alice.

Discuss and Decide

In what ways is the behavior of the March Hare and the Hatter similar?

Notes

Notes

"And be quick about it," added the Hatter, "or you'll be asleep again before it's done."

"Once upon a time there were three little sisters," the Dormouse began in a great hurry, "and their names were Elsie, Lacie, and Tillie; and they lived at the bottom of a well—"

"What did they live on?" said Alice, who always took a great interest in questions of eating and drinking.

"They lived on syrup," said the Dormouse, after thinking a minute or two.

"They couldn't have done that, you know," Alice gently remarked; "they'd have been ill."

"So they were," said the Dormouse; "*very* ill."

Alice tried a little to fancy to herself what such an extraordinary way of living would be like, but it puzzled her too much; so she went on, "But why did they live at the bottom of a well?"

"Take some more tea," the March Hare said to Alice, very earnestly.

"I've had nothing yet," Alice replied in an offended tone, "so I can't take more."

"You mean you can't take *less*," said the Hatter; "it's very easy to take *more* than nothing."

"Nobody asked *your* opinion," said Alice.

"Who's making personal remarks now?" the Hatter asked triumphantly.

Alice did not quite know what to say to this; so she helped herself to some tea and bread-and-butter, and then turned to the Dormouse, and repeated her question. "Why did they live at the bottom of a well?"

The Dormouse again took a minute or two to think about it, and then said, "It was a syrup-well."

"There's no such thing!" Alice was beginning very angrily; but the Hatter and the March Hare went "Sh! sh!" and the Dormouse sulkily remarked, "If you can't be civil, you'd better finish the story for yourself."

"No, please go on!" Alice said very humbly. "I won't interrupt you again. I dare say there may be *one*."

"One, indeed!" said the Dormouse indignantly. However, he consented to go on. "And so these three sisters—they were learning to draw, you know—"

"What did they draw?" said Alice, quite forgetting her promise.

"Syrup," said the Dormouse, without considering at all this time.

"I want a clean cup," interrupted the Hatter, "let's all move one place on."

He moved on as he spoke, and the Dormouse followed him; the March Hare moved into the Dormouse's place, and Alice rather unwillingly took the place of the March Hare. The Hatter was the only one who got any advantage from the change; and Alice was a good deal worse off than before, as the March Hare had just upset the milk-jug into his plate.

Discuss and Decide

Why does Alice keep interrupting the Dormouse?

Notes

Notes

Alice did not wish to offend the Dormouse again, so she began very cautiously, "But I don't understand. Where did they draw the syrup from?"

"You can draw water out of a water-well," said the Hatter; "so I think you could draw syrup out of a syrup-well—eh, stupid!?"

"But they were *in* the well," Alice said to the Dormouse, not choosing to notice this last remark.

"Of course they were," said the Dormouse; "—well in."

This answer so confused poor Alice that she let the Dormouse go on for some time without interrupting it.

"They were learning to draw," the Dormouse went on, yawning and rubbing its eyes, for it was getting very sleepy; "and they drew all manner of things—everything that begins with an M—"

"Why with an M?" said Alice.

"Why not?" said the March Hare.

Alice was silent.

The Dormouse had closed its eyes by this time, and was going off into a doze; but on being pinched by the Hatter, it woke up again with a little shriek, and went on, "That begins with an M, such as mouse-traps and the moon and memory and muchness—you know you say things are 'much of a muchness'—did you ever see such a thing as a drawing of a muchness?"

"Really, now you ask me," said Alice, very much confused, "I don't think—"

"Then you shouldn't talk," said the Hatter.

This piece of rudeness was more than Alice could bear; she got up in great disgust, and walked off. The Dormouse fell asleep instantly; and neither of the others took the least notice of her going, though she looked back once or twice, half hoping that they would call after her; the last time she saw them, they were trying to put the Dormouse into the teapot.

"At any rate I'll never go *there* again!" said Alice as she picked her way through the wood. "It's the stupidest tea-party I ever was at in all my life!"

Close Read

What reasons does Alice have for deciding to never go to the tea party again? Cite evidence from the text in your response.

Notes

Analyze a Student Model

Read Guy's literary response closely. The red side notes are the comments that his teacher, Ms. Jefferson, wrote.

Guy Brown

February 18

A Balancing Act

Lewis Carroll has populated his mad tea-party with a perfect balance of characters. Each one needs the others, and the way they bounce off each other allows this funny story to work.

You're right! An author plays the characters against each other.

As well as seeming quite crazy, the Hatter and the March Hare have similar personalities. They are argumentative and they are quick and clever with words. They like bullying others. But they need someone to argue with and someone to bully.

This is where the Dormouse fits in. The Hatter and the March Hare pick on him, but unlike Alice, he is still part of the club. He may be bullied, but he and his two friends seem to support each other. The Dormouse is so sleepy all the time that he doesn't seem to notice when he is pinched or ordered around.

nice point about Alice not being in the club

The fourth character in this mix is Alice. She has been brought up to be a polite girl. Even when she says "You should learn not to make personal remarks, it's very rude," the reader knows that it's something that she was taught. She can get a bit angry, but it mostly comes from being baffled by the Hatter and the March Hare. That is when she fights back. And without her, the Hatter and the March Hare would quickly get boring. They need a target, and they taunt Alice at every chance. Alice encourages them by joining the argument.

The Hatter and the Hare could get really annoying on their own!

The interaction among these four characters makes the story move along and provides a lot of humor. Without the differences in their natures, the story would either be dull or silly to the point where it wouldn't be interesting anymore.

Good ideas, well-thought-out, Guy

Discuss and Decide

What is Guy's main idea in his response to "A Mad Tea-Party"? How does he support his main idea with examples from the text?

Responding to Literature

Literary elements such as characters, settings, and events work together to make a story. After you read, you may be asked to explain how these elements shape a story and how they interact.

Are the story's **characters** believable? Do they talk and act in their own individual ways?

Can a reader picture the story's **setting**? Do the place and time add to the mood and impact events?

Are the story's **events** convincing results of interactions among the characters and the setting?

Essay Tips

Writing a Response to Literature

- Capture your ideas in a strong opening statement.
- Quote from the text to support your ideas.
- Explain how story elements work together.

Look back through "A Mad Tea-Party." Find an example of a misunderstanding between Alice and another character. Write two details from the text that reflect this misunderstanding below.

Step 2 **Practice the Task**

How does point of view influence the way events are described?

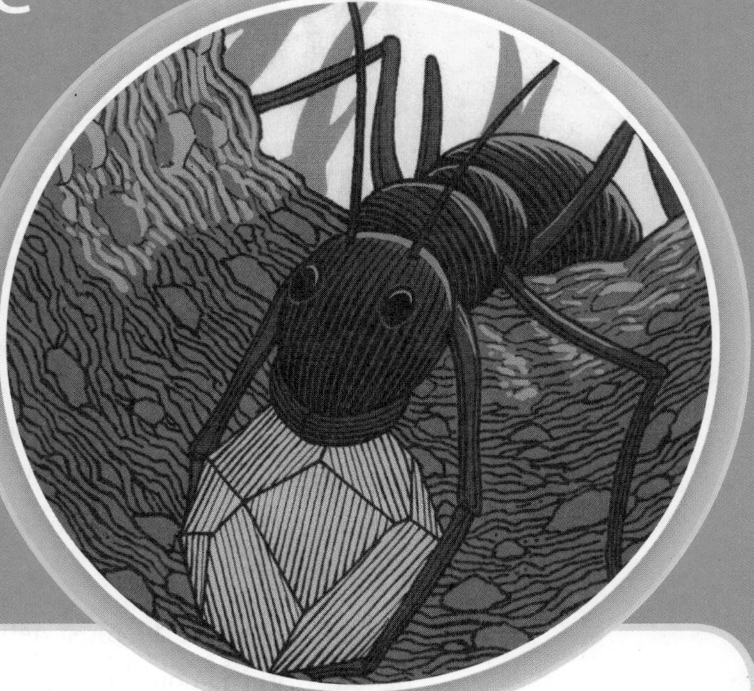

You will read:

- **A Short Story**
  Two Bad Ants

You will write:

- **A Response to Literature**
  How does point of view influence the way events are described?

Source: Short Story

AS YOU READ You will write a response to the short story below. Underline details in the text where a description reflects the ants' point of view.

Two Bad Ants

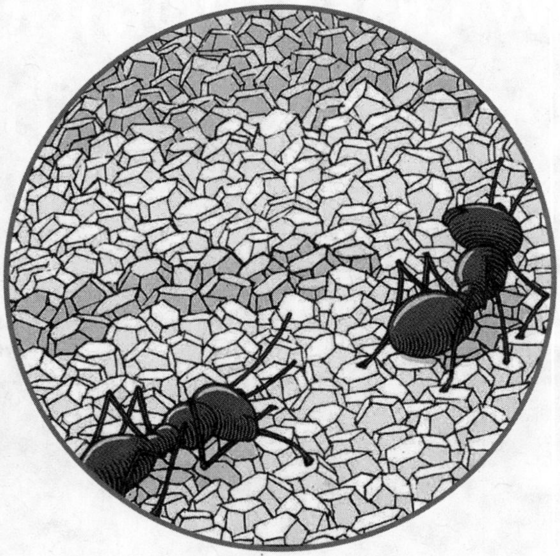

by Chris Van Allsburg

The news traveled swiftly through the tunnels of the ant world. A scout had returned with a remarkable discovery—a beautiful sparkling crystal. When the scout presented the crystal to the ant queen she took a small bite, then quickly ate the entire thing.

She deemed it the most delicious food she had ever tasted. Nothing could make her happier than to have more, much more. The ants understood. They were eager to gather more crystals because the queen was the mother of them all. Her happiness made the whole ant nest a happy place.

It was late in the day when they departed. Long shadows stretched over the entrance to the ant kingdom. One by one the insects climbed out, following the scout, who had made it clear—there were many crystals where the first had been found, but the journey was long and dangerous.

They marched into the woods that surrounded their underground home. Dusk turned to twilight, twilight to night. The path they followed twisted and turned, every bend leading them deeper into the dark forest.

More than once the line of ants stopped and anxiously listened for the sounds of hungry spiders. But all they heard was the call of crickets echoing through the woods like distant thunder.

Dew formed on the leaves above. Without warning, huge cold drops fell on the marching ants. A firefly passed overhead that, for an instant, lit up the woods with a blinding flash of blue-green light.

Discuss and Decide

From the ants' point of view, they travel through a forest. How would a human being describe this forest? Explain.

At the edge of the forest stood a mountain. The ants looked up and could not see its peak. It seemed to reach right to the heavens. But they did not stop. Up the side they climbed, higher and higher.

The wind whistled through the cracks of the mountain's face. The ants could feel its force bending their delicate antennae. Their legs grew weak as they struggled upward. At last they reached a ledge and crawled through a narrow tunnel.

When the ants came out of the tunnel they found themselves in a strange world. Smells they had known all their lives, smells of dirt and grass and rotting plants, had vanished. There was no more wind and, most puzzling of all, it seemed that the sky was gone.

They crossed smooth shiny surfaces, then followed the scout up a glassy, curved wall. They had reached their goal. From the top of the wall they looked below to a sea of crystals. One by one the ants climbed down into the sparkling treasure.

Quickly they each chose a crystal, then turned to start the journey home. There was something about this unnatural place that made the ants nervous. In fact they left in such a hurry that none of them noticed the two small ants who stayed behind.

"Why go back?" one asked the other. "This place may not feel like home, but look at all these crystals." "You're right," said the other, "we can stay here and eat this tasty treasure every day, forever." So the two ants ate crystal after crystal until they were too full to move, and fell asleep.

Daylight came. The sleeping ants were unaware of changes taking place in their new found home. A giant silver scoop hovered above them, then plunged deep into the crystals. It shoveled up both ants and crystals and carried them high into the air.

The ants were wide awake when the scoop turned, dropping them from a frightening height. They tumbled through space in a shower of crystals and fell into a boiling brown lake.

Then the giant scoop stirred violently back and forth. Crushing waves fell over the ants. They paddled hard to keep their tiny heads above water. But the scoop kept spinning the hot brown liquid.

Around and around it went, creating a whirlpool that sucked the ants deeper and deeper. They both held their breath and finally bobbed to the surface, gasping for air and spitting mouthfuls of the terrible, bitter water.

Close Read

Reread lines 50–56. What is the glassy, curved wall? Cite text evidence in your response.

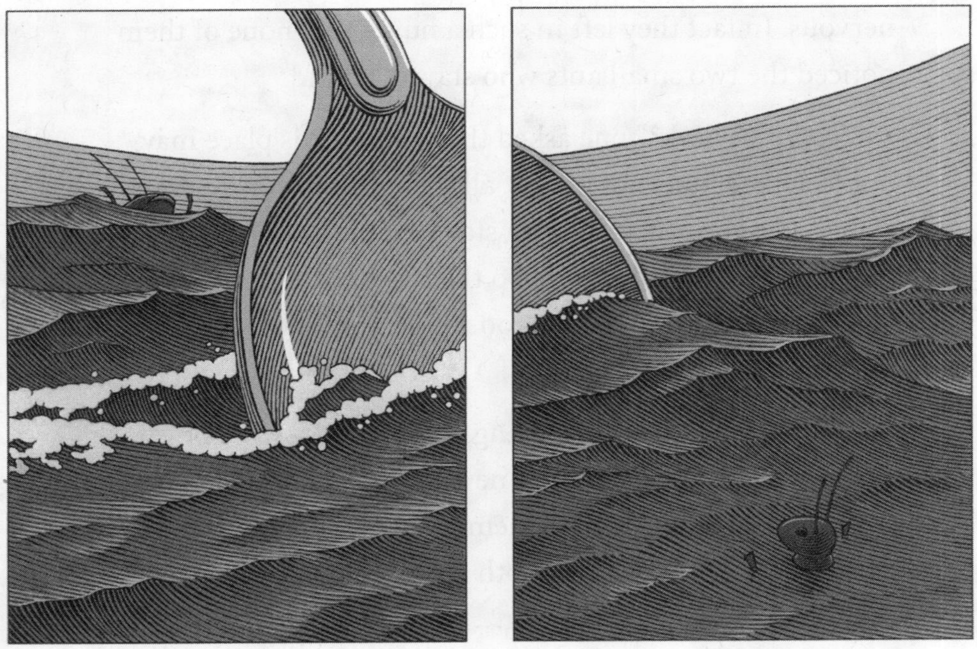

Then the lake tilted and began to empty into a cave. The ants could hear the rushing water and felt themselves pulled toward the pitch black hole. Suddenly the cave disappeared and the lake became calm. The ants swam to the shore and found that the lake had steep sides.

They hurried down the walls that held back the lake. The frightened insects looked for a place to hide, worried that the giant scoop might shovel them up again. Close by they found a huge round disk with holes that could neatly hide them.

But as soon as they had climbed inside, their hiding place was lifted, tilted, and lowered into a dark space. When the ants climbed out of the holes they were surrounded by a strange red glow. It seemed to them that every second the temperature was rising.

It soon became so unbearably hot that they thought they would soon be cooked. But suddenly the disk they were standing on rocketed upward, and the two hot ants went flying through the air.

They landed near what seemed to be a fountain—a waterfall pouring from a silver tube. Both ants had a powerful thirst and longed to dip their feverish heads into the refreshing water. They quickly climbed along the tube.

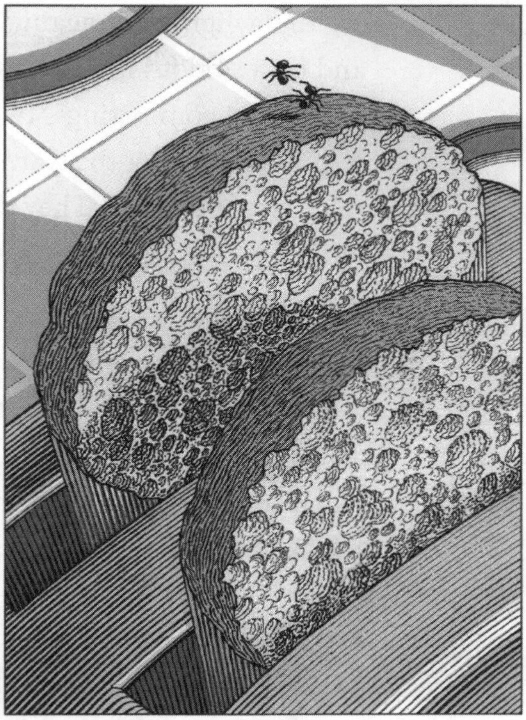

As they got closer to the rushing water the ants felt a cool spray. They tightly gripped the shiny surface of the fountain and slowly leaned their heads into the falling stream. But the force of the water was much too strong.

The tiny insects were pulled off the fountain and plunged down into a wet, dark chamber. They landed on half-eaten fruit and other soggy things. Suddenly the air was filled with loud, frightening sounds. The chamber began to spin.

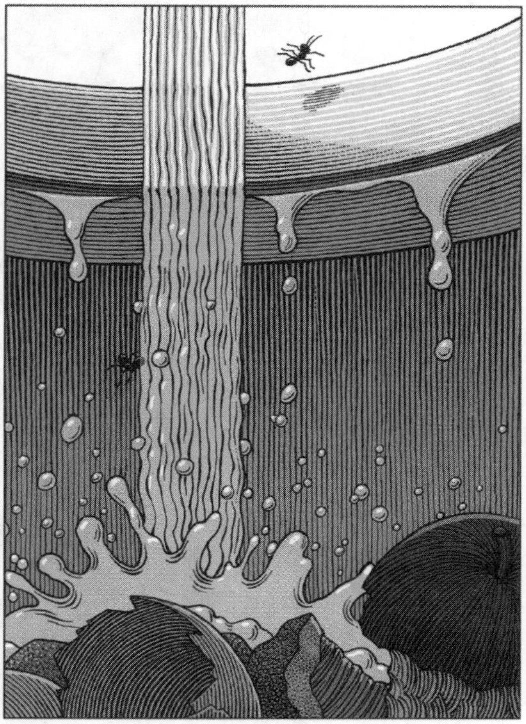

The ants were caught in a whirling storm of shredded food and stinging rain. Then, just as quickly as it had started, the noise and spinning stopped. Bruised and dizzy, the ants climbed out of the chamber.

Discuss and Decide

What reactions do the ants have to their experiences as their surroundings change?

In daylight once again, they raced through puddles and up a smooth metal wall. In the distance they saw something comforting—two long, narrow holes that reminded them of the warmth and safety of their old underground home. They climbed up into the dark openings.

But there was no safety inside these holes. A strange force passed through the wet ants. They were stunned senseless and blown out of the holes like bullets from a gun. When they landed the tiny insects were too exhausted to go on. They crawled into a dark corner and fell fast asleep.

Night had returned when the battered ants awoke to a familiar sound—the footsteps of their fellow insects returning for more crystals. They two ants slipped quietly to the end of the line. They climbed the glassy wall and once again stood amid the treasure. But this time they each chose a single crystal and followed their friends home.

Standing at the edge of their ant hole, the two ants listened to the joyful sounds that came from below. They knew how grateful their mother queen would be when they gave her their crystals. At that moment, the two ants felt happier than they'd ever felt before. This was their home, this was their family. This was where they were meant to be.

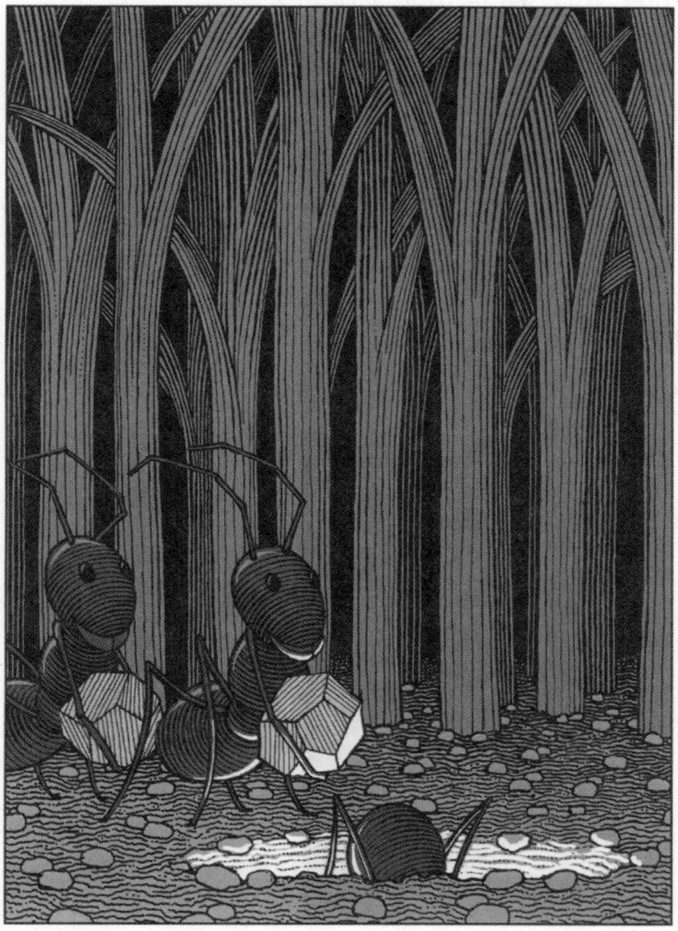

Discuss and Decide

Why are the ants happy to be home?

Respond to Questions

These questions will help you think about the source you've read. Use your notes and refer to the source to answer the questions. Your answers to these questions will help you write your essay.

1. What does the word *anxiously* mean in line 20?

   a. closely

   b. nervously

   c. slowly

   d. constantly

2. Why do the two ants decide not to return with the others?

   a. There are many of the tasty crystals there to eat.

   b. They are too afraid to go back home.

   c. They are still hungry.

   d. The place where the crystals are feels like home.

3. Look at lines 119–130. From the ants' point of view, they fall into a "wet, dark chamber" where they are "caught in a whirling storm of shredded food and stinging rain." What would a human being call this place?

   a. a coffee mug

   b. a cave

   c. a garbage disposal

   d. a toaster

4 **Prose Constructed-Response** How does the ants' experience inside the toaster reflect their unique point of view? Cite text evidence in your response.

5 **Prose Constructed-Response** Recall when the ants climbed into the two holes in the walls. How are the holes different from what the ants expected? Cite text evidence in your response.

amble
tamble

The ants expected the 2 holes to be safe like their underground house, but it was the actual opposite. They were blown out of the holes, feeling the force as for a bullet.

6 **Prose Constructed-Response** How might the account of the mountain and the ledge in lines 28–43 be different if it were described from the point of view of humans instead of ants?

Planning and Prewriting

Assignment

Write a response to literature to answer the question: How does point of view influence the way events are described?

Before you draft your essay, complete some important planning steps.

Before you start writing, determine your main idea. Think about the ants' point of view of events in the story and consider how a human being's point of view of events would be different. Look for supporting details to include in your essay. Complete the chart below to help you think about the way different events in the story might be perceived.

You may prefer to plan on a computer.

Point of View

Ants' Point of View	Person's Point of View
a mountain at the edge of a forest	the wall of a house next to a lawn
crystals	a sugar bowl
a boiling brown lake	dirty sink water
a round disk with holes lowered into a dark, hot place that glows red	spoon
silver water	water faucet
hole	wall outlet

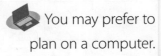

Finalize Your Plan

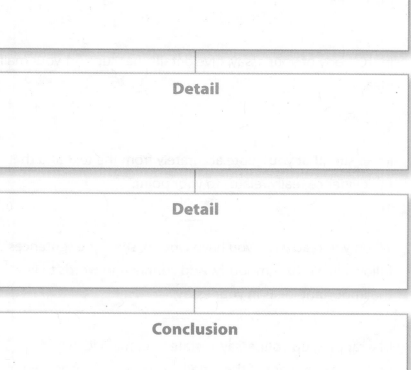

You know what you want to say in your response to the short story. Now, it's time to plan the structure of your essay. You will save time and create a more organized, logical essay by planning the structure before you start writing.

Use your responses and notes from pp. 92–94 to complete the graphic organizer.

Introduction

From the 2 bads

◀ State your main idea and what you will be comparing and contrasting. Think about including an interesting question or vivid image to grab your reader's attention.

Detail

◀ Give details in each paragraph to support your main idea. You might want to compare and contrast the subjects one point at a time.

Detail

Detail

Conclusion

◀ Restate your main idea and details. Try to include an additional insight that follows from your main idea.

Draft Your Essay

If you drafted your essay on the computer, you may wish to print it out.

As you write, think about:

- **Purpose** *to discuss point of view in a response to literature*
- **Clarity** *ideas that are straightforward and understandable*
- **Support** *examples from the sources that support your ideas*
- **Organization** *the logical structure for your essay*
- **Connecting Words** *words that link your ideas*

Revision Checklist: Self-Evaluation

Use the checklist below to guide your self-evaluation.

Ask Yourself	Make It Better
1. Does the introduction grab the audience's attention and state your main idea?	A great introduction hooks your audience. Start with a question or a vivid image. Make sure you clearly state your main idea.
2. Do the details support your main idea?	In the body of your essay, give details that support your main idea.
3. Is your evidence accurate and relevant?	Make sure that you quote accurately from the text and that the evidence really relates to your point.
4. Does your essay flow well and connect the details to your main idea?	When you read what you have written, see if the sentences follow each other smoothly. Add connecting words to link the important ideas in your essay.
5. Does the last section restate your main idea?	In wrapping up your essay, restate your main idea and provide a summary of the details you gave to support your main idea.

Revision Checklist: Peer Review

Exchange your essay with a classmate, or read it aloud to your partner. As you read and comment on your partner's essay, focus on organization and evidence. Help your partner find parts of the draft that need to be revised.

What to Look For	Notes for My Partner
1. Does the introduction grab the audience's attention and state the main idea?	
2. Do the details support the main idea?	
3. Is the evidence accurate and relevant?	
4. Does the essay flow well and connect the details to the main idea?	
5. Does the last section restate the main idea?	

Support Your Ideas!

Review Your Use of Text Evidence

When you write a response to literature, the best way to support your ideas is to cite evidence from the literature itself. You can use quotes, give examples from the text, or tell what the characters say, think, or feel.

This paragraph was written about *Two Bad Ants*. There is no direct evidence from the source material, but there is a lot of the writer's opinion.

Ants and people both like sugar. But the two bad ants don't realize that the crystals are actually just sugar in a bowl. They're not very smart because people can understand that right away. If they realized that, they wouldn't have been shocked when the spoon came down into the sugar bowl and scooped them up.

The paragraph can be improved by using quotes from the source to support the writer's idea.

The ants in this story like sugar and the ant queen calls it "the most delicious food she had ever tasted." However, the tiny ants see a sugar bowl as a "sea of crystals." They are not used to this "strange world" inside the house. So, when a spoon picks up some sugar from the bowl, the ants think it is a "giant scoop" and their surprise causes them to become "wide awake."

Essay Tips

Cite from the Source

- State your ideas clearly, with no room for confusion.
- Support your ideas with evidence from the source material.
- Don't use unsupported opinions or assume that your audience already knows all the information that you know.

Edit

Edit your essay to correct spelling, grammar, and punctuation errors.

Step 3 **Perform the Task**

How can a narrator shape the way events are presented?

You will read:

- **A Short Story**
  The True Story of the Three Little Pigs

You will write:

- **A Response to Literature**
  How can a narrator shape the way events are presented?

Source: Short Story

AS YOU READ

Think about the differences you find between the familiar story of the Three Little Pigs and this telling from the wolf's perspective. Make notes about the wolf's presentation of events.

Notes

The True Story of the Three Little Pigs

by Jon Scieszka • illustrated by Lane Smith

Everybody knows the story of the Three Little Pigs. Or at least they think they do. But I'll let you in on a little secret. Nobody knows the real story, because nobody has ever heard *my* side of the story.

I'm the wolf. Alexander T. Wolf.

You can call me Al.

I don't know how this whole Big Bad Wolf thing got started, but it's all wrong.

Maybe it's because of our diet.

Hey, it's not my fault wolves eat cute little animals like bunnies and sheep and pigs. That's just the way we are. If cheeseburgers were cute, folks would probably think you were Big and Bad, too.

But like I was saying, the whole Big Bad Wolf thing is all wrong. The real story is about a sneeze and a cup of sugar.

This is the real story.

Way back in Once Upon a Time time, I was making a birthday cake for my dear old granny.

I had a terrible sneezing cold.

I ran out of sugar.

So I walked down the street to ask my neighbor for a cup of sugar. Now this neighbor was a pig.

And he wasn't too bright, either.

He had built his whole house out of straw.

Can you believe it? I mean who in his right mind would build a house of straw?

Discuss and Decide

Does the wolf think that he has done something wrong? How can you tell?

Notes

Notes

So of course the minute I knocked on the door, it fell right in. I didn't want to just walk into someone else's house. So I called, "Little Pig, Little Pig, are you in?" No answer.

I was just about to go home without the cup of sugar for my dear old granny's birthday cake.

That's when my nose started to itch.

I felt a sneeze coming on.

Well I huffed.

And I snuffed.

And I sneezed a great sneeze.

And you know what? That whole darn straw house fell down. And right in the middle of the pile of straw was the First Little Pig—dead as a doornail.

He had been home the whole time.

It seemed like a shame to leave a perfectly good ham dinner lying there in the straw. So I ate it up.

Think of it as a big cheeseburger just lying there.

I was feeling a little better. But I still didn't have my cup of sugar. So I went to the next neighbor's house.

This neighbor was the First Little Pig's brother.

He was a little smarter, but not much.

He had built his house of sticks.

I rang the bell on the stick house.

Nobody answered.

I called, "Mr. Pig, Mr. Pig, are you in?"

He yelled back, "Go away wolf. You can't come in. I'm shaving the hairs on my chinny chin chin."

I had just grabbed the doorknob when I felt another sneeze coming on.

I huffed. And I snuffed. And I tried to cover my mouth, but I sneezed a great sneeze.

And you're not going to believe it, but this guy's house fell down just like his brother's.

When the dust cleared, there was the Second Little Pig—dead as a doornail. Wolf's honor.

Now you know food will spoil if you just leave it out in the open. So I did the only thing there was to do. I had dinner again. Think of it as a second helping. I was getting awfully full. But my cold was feeling a little better. And I still didn't have that cup of sugar for my dear old granny's birthday cake. So I went to the next house. This guy was

Discuss and Decide

According to the wolf, why did he eat the First Little Pig?

Notes

Notes

the First and Second Little Pigs' brother. He must have been the brains of the family. He had built his house of bricks.

I knocked on the brick house. No answer.

I called "Mr. Pig, Mr. Pig, are you in?"

And do you know what that rude little porker answered?

"Get out of here, Wolf. Don't bother me again."

Talk about impolite!

He probably had a whole sackful of sugar.

And he wouldn't give me even one little cup for my dear sweet old granny's birthday cake.

What a pig!

I was just about to go home and maybe make a nice birthday card instead of a cake, when I felt my cold coming on.

I huffed.

And I snuffed.

And I sneezed once again.

Then the Third Little Pig yelled, "And your old granny can sit on a pin!"

Now I'm usually a pretty calm fellow. But when somebody talks about my granny like that, I go a little crazy.

Close Read

Find two examples that reveal the Wolf's feelings toward the Third Little Pig. Cite text evidence in your response.

Notes

Notes

When the cops drove up, of course I was trying to break down this Pig's door. And the whole time I was huffing and puffing and sneezing and making a real scene.

The rest, as they say, is history.

The news reporters found out about the two pigs I had for dinner. They figured a sick guy going to borrow a cup of sugar didn't sound very exciting. So they jazzed up the story with all of that "Huff and puff and blow your house down." And they made me the Big Bad Wolf.

That's it.

The real story. I was framed.

But maybe you could loan me a cup of sugar.

Respond to Questions

These questions will help you think about the source you've read. Use your notes and refer to the source to answer the questions. Your answers to these questions will help you write your essay.

1. Which sentence from the text explains the Wolf's reason for eating the First Little Pig?
   a. "Hey, it's not my fault wolves eat cute little animals . . ."
   b. "I mean who in his right mind would build a house of straw?"
   c. "It seemed like a shame to leave a perfectly good ham dinner lying there in the straw."
   d. "But when somebody talks about my granny like that, I go a little crazy."

2. Why did the wolf say he blew down the houses of the first two pigs?
   a. He wanted to eat the pigs.
   b. He had a cold and couldn't stop himself from sneezing.
   c. He wanted to borrow a cup of sugar.
   d. He was proving that they were not very smart.

3. What difference was there between the Wolf's visits to the First Little Pig and to the Second Little Pig?
   a. The First Little Pig didn't say a word to the Wolf.
   b. The Wolf sneezed the Second Little Pig's house down.
   c. The Second Little Pig's door just fell right in.
   d. The Wolf blew the First Little Pig's house down on purpose.

4. What is a claim you could make about the wolf's point of view in *The True Story of the Three Little Pigs?*

   a. The wolf is sorry that he tried to eat the pigs.

   b. The wolf doesn't think that he did anything wrong.

   c. The wolf went to each pig's house to blow it down.

   d. The wolf was just trying to eat some cheeseburgers.

5. **Prose Constructed-Response** What is the "real" story of the Three Little Pigs according to the wolf? Cite text evidence in your response.

6. **Prose Constructed-Response** How would a pig's explanation differ from the Wolf's explanation of why he ate the pigs?

7. **Prose Constructed-Response** Is the Wolf a convincing narrator whose retelling a reader can trust? Cite text evidence in your response.

Write the Essay

Read the assignment.

> **Assignment**
> You have read *The True Story of the Three Little Pigs*. Write a response to literature that explains how the narrator shapes the way events are presented in the story. Organize your essay using main idea and details. Cite text evidence from what you have read.

Plan

Use the graphic organizer to help you outline the structure of your response to literature.

Introduction

◀ Identify the main idea of your essay. Include an interesting detail, question, or quotation to hook your audience.

Detail

◀ Organize each of your points in a way that makes sense. Each paragraph should give details that support the main idea you presented in the introduction.

Detail

Detail

Conclusion

◀ Restate your main idea, and try to include a further insight or observation.

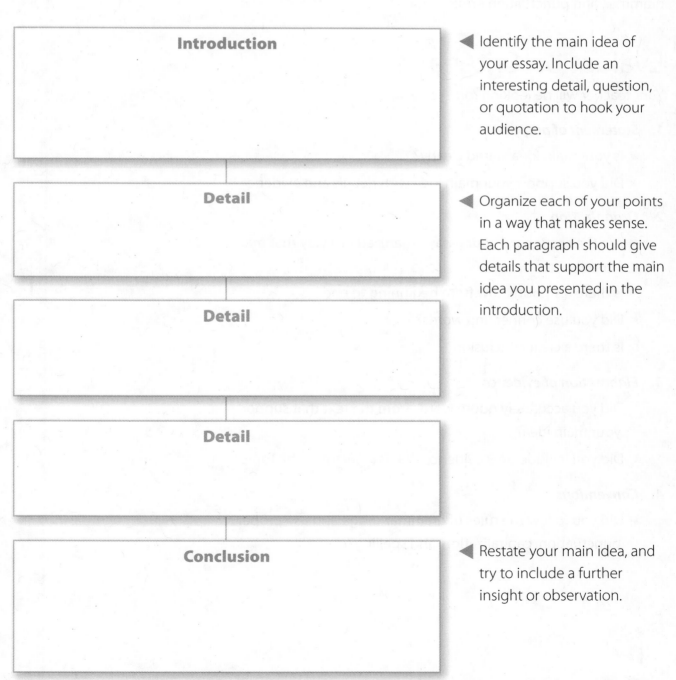

Draft

Use your notes and completed graphic organizer to write a first draft of your response to literature.

Revise and Edit

Look back over your essay and compare it to the Evaluation Criteria. Revise your essay and edit it to correct spelling, grammar, and punctuation errors.

You may wish to draft and edit your essay on the computer.

Evaluation Criteria

Your teacher will be looking for:

1. ***Statement of purpose***
   - Is your main idea stated clearly?
   - Did you support your main idea with details and evidence?
2. ***Organization***
   - Are the sections of your essay organized in a way that makes sense?
   - Is there a smooth flow from beginning to end?
   - Did you use connecting words?
   - Is there a clear conclusion?
3. ***Elaboration of evidence***
   - Did you accurately quote words from the text that support your main idea?
   - Did you include only evidence that is relevant to the topic?
4. ***Conventions***
   - Did you follow the rules of grammar usage and use proper punctuation, capitalization, and spelling?

Surprising Meetings

Unit 4

Narrative

Step 1 Analyze the Model

Evaluate a narrative about what happens when Albert Einstein and Harry Houdini meet.

Step 2 Practice the Task

Write a story about what happens when superheroes compete at a school field day.

Step 3 Perform the Task

Write a narrative about what happens when you realize you're not alone during an overnight stay in a strange house.

A narrative might be a true account or a fictional story. Whether it is true or not, a narrative must be believable. Factual details can help a story seem credible. On the other hand, details that are not factual can make a story seem unrealistic. For example, a science fiction story that takes place on Mars won't be believable if its description of Mars includes trees and beaches.

A fictional narrative might get its start from an original idea that an author read about. The ideas often come from informational sources such as news articles, biographies, scientific writing, and maps. The writer then uses information from the sources for inspiration. Information from a variety of sources might be combined with the author's imagination to create a compelling story.

As you read from sources and write fictional narratives of your own, remember that getting the facts right is a key to writing good fiction. It gives your writing a foundation and it gives readers an engaging, believable story.

IN THIS UNIT, you will evaluate a story about what happens when two famous people from history meet. Then you will read two sources and write a story about what happens when people with superhuman abilities enter a sports competition. Finally, you will read two sources and write a story about an unexpected encounter in an unfamiliar place.

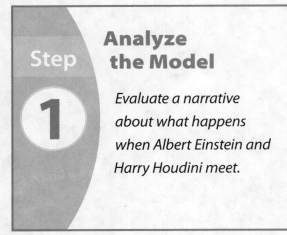

Step 1 **Analyze the Model**

What happens when Houdini meets Einstein?

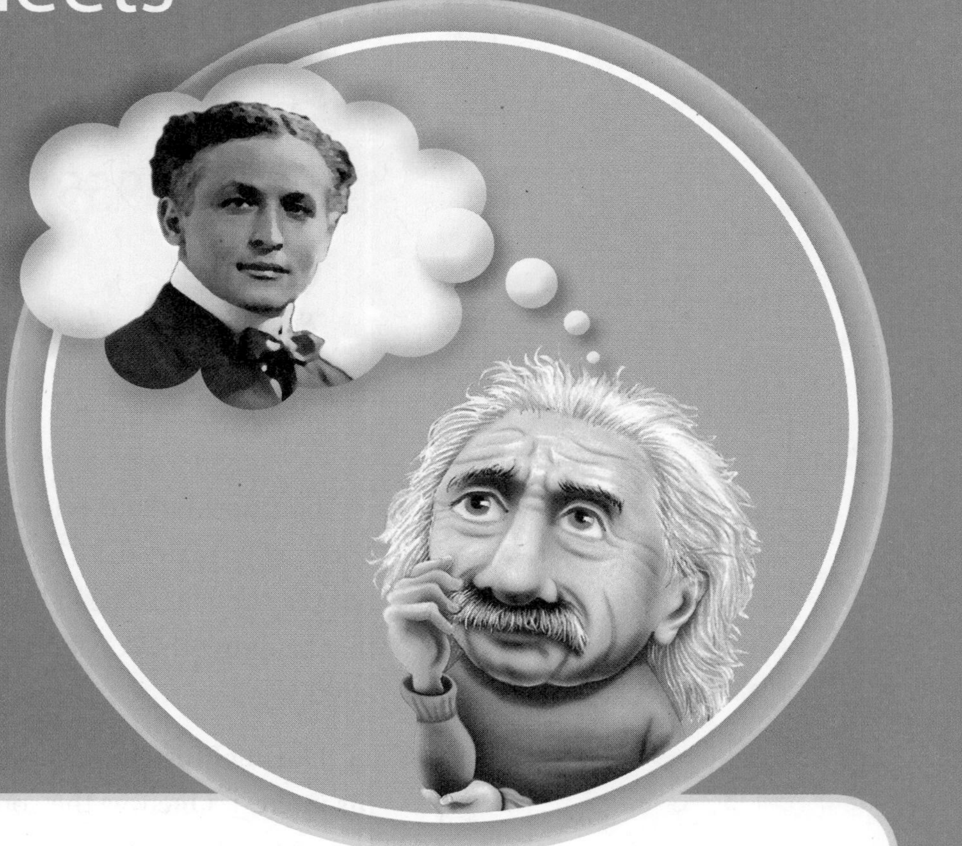

You will read:

- **Two Biographies**

  Albert Einstein (1879–1955)

  Harry Houdini (1874–1926)

You will analyze:

- **A Student Model**

  When Harry Met Albert

Source 1: Biography

Mr. Kim's student, Jane York, read the following two sources for her narrative about an imaginary meeting between Albert Einstein and Harry Houdini. (Einstein visited New York City in April, 1921; Houdini lived in New York City at that time.) As you read, make notes in the side columns and underline useful information.

Notes

Albert Einstein
(1879–1955)

"Science is a wonderful thing if one does not have to earn one's living at it."

The most famous scientist of the 20th century was born in Germany in 1879. As a child in school, he was not very notable. One of his teachers even remarked that he didn't think Albert Einstein would ever achieve anything.

During Einstein's childhood, two "wonders" sparked his interest. One was the compass. At the age of five, he became intrigued by the invisible force that controlled the compass needle. The other wonder was a geometry book that he read at the age of twelve!

Einstein went to university in Switzerland, but first had to catch up on the subjects that were not math or physics. He graduated in 1900, and could not find work

Notes

until he landed a job at the Swiss patent office. There, he did the work fast enough to give himself plenty of time to think—and Einstein could spend years thinking about ideas that most people would ignore. After struggling to explain light for ten years, he finally published work that gained him recognition.

Einstein became a famous physicist, lecturing around the world, and he won the Nobel Prize in 1921. He was a director of physics at the University of Berlin, but with the rise of the Nazi party, he decided to leave Germany forever in 1932. (There was also a price on his head!)

Einstein was welcomed to the United States, where he became the star among other extraordinarily gifted scientists at the Institute for Advanced Study in Princeton, New Jersey. When his work was used to help develop the atomic bomb, though, he was horrified. He was personally not involved in the project.

Einstein continued his research, but never managed to discover what he dreamed of: a theory that would explain how all of the forces in the universe worked together.

Source 2: Biography

Notes

Harry Houdini

(1874–1926)

"What the eyes see and the ears hear, the mind believes."

He was born in 1874 as Erik Weisz, but he would later be known all over the world by a single name: Houdini.

Weisz moved from Hungary to the United States when he was a very young child. In New York City, at the age of 17, he started a magic act and began calling himself Harry Houdini. Two years later he replaced his partner with his wife Bess, who he had married after knowing her for only three weeks. The couple's act was known as "The Houdinis."

Over the next few years, Houdini performed in vaudeville shows, building up his new identity as an escape artist. It took nearly five discouraging years until he got his big break, but then his career took off. Houdini became wildly popular around the country, and toured Europe as "The King of Handcuffs."

Houdini kept introducing new daredevil escapes into his act: he escaped jail, jumped handcuffed from bridges, and then came up with his famous milk-can escape. In this act, the handcuffed Houdini squeezed himself into a metal milk can that was filled with water. The lid was closed and padlocked shut, and a curtain was closed to conceal the can. After a little more than two minutes, Houdini emerged from behind the curtain, out of breath and soaking wet.

Houdini's escapes mystified his audiences. He would typically be chained and shackled, locked into a box, and submerged underwater. Or he might be suspended by his feet 75 feet above the ground, and still manage to get free.

There was no "magic" in Houdini's act, and he spent a lot of time revealing the tricks of those who claimed special powers. Houdini was a great showman, he was incredibly strong and agile, and he was an expert with all kinds of locks. He also designed (with crafty features) many of the devices from which he escaped.

Close Read

What might Einstein ask Houdini about if he were to meet him? Cite evidence from the text.

Notes

Analyze a Student Model

After the class read the biographies, Mr. Kim asked his students to write a narrative about an imaginary meeting between the two men. Read Jane's story closely. The red notes are the comments that Mr. Kim wrote.

Jane York

June 21

When Harry Met Albert

The people on the sidewalk whispered excitedly to each other, pointing at the wild-haired man walking toward the entrance of the hotel. His clothes were rumpled and his mustache looked crooked. A photographer took a picture. The man made his way into the hotel.

These details will grab the reader's interest!

Inside, a man struggled wildly with the chains and locks that bound him to a chair. Seconds later, he shucked off his shackles and stood up, smiling. "Professor Einstein," he said, "So glad you came!"

"Up to your usual tricks, eh, Mr. Houdini?" remarked the professor.

The dialogue adds humor to the story.

Houdini laughed. "The hotel manager bet me that I couldn't get out of those chains. Guess I won the bet," he said, straightening his tie. "But enough of all that. I really wanted to meet you, Professor, ever since I started following your research. You can count me as one of your greatest admirers."

"I have been following your work, too, Mr. Houdini," replied Einstein. "So, how do you get out of that milk can?"

Including actual details about their lives makes your story more credible.

"The same way I get in, Professor, but in reverse," said Houdini.

"In other words," said Einstein, "I will never know."

"Probably not. But that's what keeps us at the top, right?" answered Houdini. "Nobody can understand what either of us does."

Funny ending! Nice wrap up.

Discuss and Decide

Give two examples of facts from the sources that Jane used in her narrative.

Set the Scene!

The setting is the time and place of the action in a story. A good writer will include memorable images and concrete details to make the setting come alive. In her story, Jane could have described the setting more realistically so that the reader could better picture where the action takes place.

Here is a part of Jane's story:

Inside, a man struggled wildly with the chains and locks that bound him to a chair.

How could Jane describe the scene better? She could supply details that let the reader "see" the setting. Here's an example:

In the hotel lobby, a well-dressed gentleman struggled wildly with the chains and locks that bound him to a handsome velvet chair.

Story Tips

Remember These Tips!

- Imagine the setting in your mind. Then, try to put it down in words. Do your words accurately describe what you are thinking of?
- Imagine that a reader will draw a picture based on your words. Would it look like the setting you are writing about?

Look back through Jane's story. Find one description of the setting that you could improve. Rewrite the description and exchange your work with a partner. Ask your partner if your writing lets him or her better imagine the setting.

Step 2 **Practice the Task**

What happens when superheroes compete at a field day?

You will read:

- **An Event Schedule**
  Jefferson Elementary Athletic Day Program
- **A Comic Book Blog**
  My New Favorite Superhero Team

You will write:

- **A Narrative**
  What happens when superheroes compete at a field day?

Source 1: Event Schedule

AS YOU READ You will write a narrative about what happens when superheroes compete at a school field day. As you read, underline information that may be useful to you when you write your story.

Jefferson Elementary
Athletic Day Program

This Saturday come down to Jefferson Elementary School for our annual Athletic Day!

Check out this year's events below.

Time	Name of Event	Description
8:00 A.M.	Registration	Make sure to get here early—registration fills up fast! Each registered participant will receive a name tag and a bottle of water.
9:00 A.M.	Hurdles	Hurdlers start by placing their feet in starting blocks—two footplates attached to a frame. Once the signal to start is given, hurdlers run down their lane, jumping over all the hurdles. Hurdlers must stay in their lanes. The winner is the hurdler who finishes in the shortest time.
10:00 A.M.	Tug of War	Each team has 5 players. The rope is marked in the center, and each team's winning point is marked on the ground. Players may not sit down while pulling, or wrap their body around the rope in any way. A team wins when they pull the center of the rope past their winning mark.

Time	Name of Event	Description
10:30 A.M..	Pull-Up Contest	How many can you do? Contestants grab the bar, hands facing away from them, arms a bit more than shoulder length apart. From a hanging position (no swinging!), they pull their chins all the away above the bar, lower themselves back down, and repeat. The person who does the most pull-ups wins.
11:00 A.M.	Three-Legged Race	Each team must have three legs to enter! Partners stand side-by-side. The right leg of one partner and the left leg of the other are tied together with scarves. Then, partners run together as fast as they can. The first team across the finish line wins.
12:00 P.M.	Relay Race	The grand finale! This race consists of four sections, each run by a different person on the team. As a runner finishes a section, he or she passes a baton to the next section's runner. The first team to complete the race wins.
1:00 P.M.	Picnic Lunch	Let's eat!

Source 2: Comic Book Blog

Home | About | Blog Life | Archive

Search This Website

My New Favorite Superhero Team

A BLOG BY SUPERFAN3000

March 7

I've really been enjoying the new Incredikids comics recently. For those who are unfamiliar, they are about three kids who sneak into a mad scientist's lab and accidentally get superpowers. Here's an introduction to the main characters!

HEROINES & HEROES

★★★★★★★★★★★★★★★

Codename: Tough Guy

Real Name: Mo Sill

Abilities: Super strength, very high endurance

Profile: Mo Sill wasn't a particularly big kid until he took a sip of what he thought was Doctor Deranged's protein shake. It turned out to be an experimental formula that made him tougher than a tank with amazing staying power. Mo uses his powers to fight crime, but still doesn't quite know his own strength—the front door to Incredikid HQ has been replaced six times just from Mo trying to turn the doorknob.

Codename: Zip Girl

Real Name: Val Ossidy

Abilities: Superhuman speed

Profile: Val gained her incredible speed when she was zapped by Doctor Deranged's High-Speed Teleportation Machine during a malfunction. Now she can jog faster than a jet can fly—without breaking a sweat. She loves running circles around evildoers, but all that quickness comes with a price: she gets motion sickness if she sprints for too long.

Codename: The Aphid Kid

Real Name: Arthur O. Pod

Abilities: Six legs, can climb walls, heightened sense of smell (thanks to antennae)

Profile: Arthur was playing around with Doctor Deranged's DNA Processor when he accidentally turned it on, trapping himself inside. A small plant-eating insect called an aphid also wandered in from the Doctor's mutant garden. When Arthur emerged from the machine, he was half human, half insect! He enjoys being able to crawl up walls, but sometimes his aphid instincts take over and he can't stop eating plants.

Close Read

Explain how Zip Girl's ability might be useful in an athletic day event.

Respond to Questions

In Step 2, you have read an event schedule and a comic book blog. Use your notes and refer to the sources as you answer the questions. Your answers will help you write your narrative.

1. Looking at "Jefferson Elementary Athletic Day Program," how are hurdles and the relay race different?

   a. Hurdles involves jumping, but the relay race involves passing a baton.

   b. Hurdles involves passing a baton, but the relay race involves jumping.

   c. Hurdles is not a race, but the relay race is.

   d. Hurdles has a winner, but the relay race does not.

2. What does the word *endurance* mean in "My New Favorite Superhero Team?"

   a. traveling at great speed

   b. the ability to keep going

   c. the outcome of an experiment

   d. being half insect and half human

3. Which detail from Source 2 describes how fast Zip Girl is?

   a. ". . . she was zapped by Doctor Deranged's High-Speed Teleportation Machine . . ."

   b. ". . . enjoys being able to crawl up walls . . ."

   c. ". . . can't stop eating plants."

   d. ". . . she can jog faster than a jet can fly—without breaking a sweat."

4 **Prose Constructed-Response** Which Incredikid would be most likely to excel at the tug of war? Use text evidence in your response.

5 **Prose Constructed-Response** Which of the Incredikids' superpowers might cause problems in the athletic day events? Use text evidence in your response.

6 **Prose Constructed-Response** What are some ways that the Incredikids could work together in field-day events requiring a team?

Planning and Prewriting

Before you draft your narrative, complete some important planning steps.

Assignment
Write a narrative about what happens when superheroes compete at a school field day.

Collect Information

You may prefer to plan on a computer.

Before you start writing, think about the sources you've read. Look for interesting facts and details that you can include in your narrative. Complete the chart below with information from each source.

Source	Interesting Facts to Use in My Narrative
Event Schedule Jefferson Elementary Athletic Day Program	
Comic Book Blog My New Favorite Superhero Team	

Finalize Your Plan

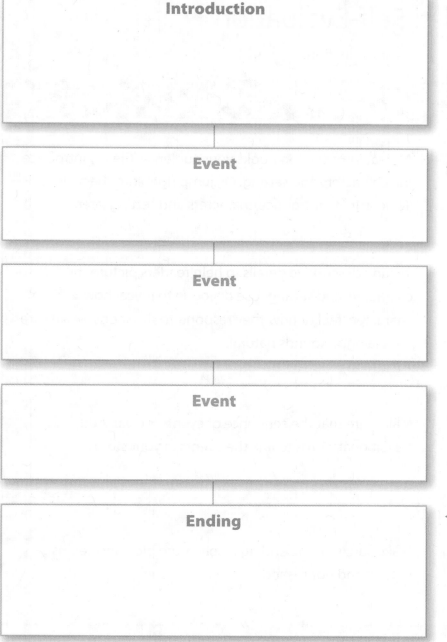

You know what you want to include in your narrative. Now, it's time to plan the structure of your story. You will save time and create a more organized, logical narrative by planning the structure before you start writing.

Use your responses and notes from pp. 126–128 to complete the graphic organizer.

Introduction

◀ Establish the setting and characters. Alternatively, you may want to jump right into the action. (If so, make sure you introduce setting and characters at some point.)

Event

◀ Develop the plot with a series of events.

Event

Event

Ending

◀ The ending should wrap up the story and resolve the plot.

Draft Your Narrative

If you drafted your story on the computer, you may wish to print it out.

As you write, think about:

- **Purpose** *to entertain or engage the reader*
- **Clarity** *straightforward, understandable ideas and descriptions*
- **Support** *factual details that help make your story believable*
- **Organization** *the logical structure for your story*
- **Connecting Words** *words that link your ideas*

Revision Checklist: Self-Evaluation

Use the checklist below to guide your self-evaluation.

Ask Yourself	Make It Better
1. Does the introduction grab your audience's attention?	A great introduction hooks your audience. Clearly introduce the characters and setting. Or, jump right into the action. (Make sure to introduce characters and setting later.)
2. Do you use dialogue and description to develop your story?	Include descriptive details to help readers picture the characters and setting. Use dialogue to reveal how characters feel or how they respond to situations. Make sure the dialogue sounds natural.
3. Are events in your story presented in a clear order?	Make sure that the sequence of events is clear. Add transitional words to link the events in your story.
4. Does your conclusion bring all the action to an end?	Make sure that the ending resolves the plot, and seems natural and not rushed.

Revision Checklist: Peer Review

Exchange your story with a classmate, or read it out loud to your partner. As you read and comment on your partner's story, focus on the elements of a good narrative. Help your partner find parts of the draft that need to be revised.

What to Look For	Notes for My Partner
1. Does the introduction grab the audience's attention?	
2. Do dialogue and description develop the story?	
3. Are events in the story presented in a clear order?	
4. Does the conclusion bring all the action to an end?	

Writing Dialogue

Dialogue is conversation between two or more characters in a story. It can be used to reveal the characters' personalities, explain situations, and move events along. It can also be used to reveal important details about those situations and events.

This example of dialogue explains a situation:

"Slow down, Zip Girl!" said Tough Guy. "You're going too fast!"

"Sorry, Tough. I'm so used to speeding toward people in need, rather than a finish line," Zip Girl reflected.

"Maybe you should save Aphid—he's grazing again," Tough Guy replied.

Story Tips

Remember These Tips When Writing Dialogue

- Words that characters say appear in quotation marks. Make sure that it's clear who is speaking.
- One character may know more about something than another character knows. Be sure your dialogue reflects the characters' knowledge of events in the story.
- Make sure the dialogue adds something to the story. It might reveal how characters feel or explain the action.

Edit

Edit your essay to correct spelling, grammar, and punctuation errors.

Step 3 **Perform the Task**

What happens when you realize you are not alone in a strange house?

You will read:

- **A Newspaper Article**
  An Adventure Right Here in Lawndale
- **A Floor Plan**
  The Home of Explorer Illinois Smith

You will write:

- **A Narrative**
  What happens when you realize you are not alone in a strange house?

Source 1: Newspaper Article

AS YOU READ
Look for information that you could use to write your narrative. Underline interesting details that could make your story more engaging. Record ideas or questions about the sources in the side margins.

Notes

An Adventure Right Here in Lawndale

by Jess Rodgers

As many residents know, the world-famous explorer Illinois Smith calls Lawndale home. Whenever Smith returns from a trip with a set of dinosaur fossils or another Egyptian mummy for his impressive collection, it ends up in his house, which is large enough to be a museum.

I visited Smith at his home early last week. Stepping inside, I looked through a window at a garden filled only with Venus fly traps. "I brought those back from the North Carolina coast," Smith told me. "I keep the bugs I feed them over in the garage."

We then walked through a large hallway, which held two massive suits of armor. "I found those while on a trip to northern France," Smith explained. "Rumor has it they're from the Battle of Agincourt in 1415. The French army wore these huge suits of armor, which made it hard for them to move. The English army was smaller, but they didn't have such heavy armor, so they were able to win the battle. Pretty neat, huh?"

We kept walking down the corridor. I thought he was going to show me his world famous mummy collection, when suddenly he said, "You probably already know all about my mummies. But did you know about this?"

He opened a door to a room filled with all sorts of machines. "These are Rube Goldberg machines," Smith said. Rube Goldberg was a cartoonist who drew complicated machines that did very simple things. For example, he drew a machine that automatically wiped a person's face after he sipped some soup with a spoon. The machine had many steps, involving a bird, a clock, and a rocket. "I have books about everything I collect, including several on Rube Goldberg machines. So, I try to build some when I'm not traveling," Smith continued. "I guess you could call it my hobby."

If you'd like to see Illinois Smith's house for yourself, he offers tours on the third Saturday of every month.

Notes

Close Read

What types of books might you expect to find in Illinois Smith's library? Cite text evidence in your response.

Source 2: Floor Plan

The Home of Explorer ILLINOIS SMITH

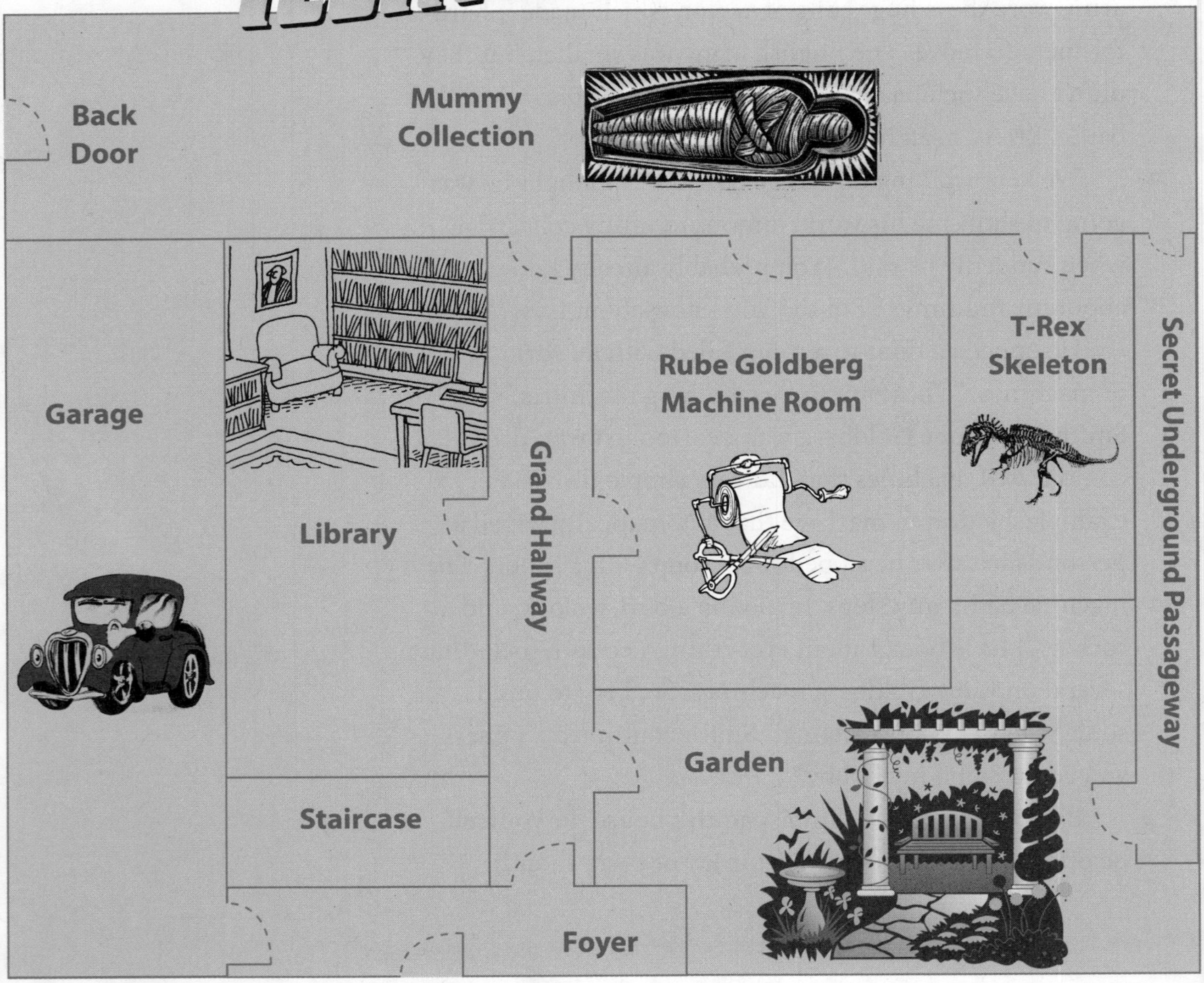

Nutcracker from the Rube Goldberg Machine Room

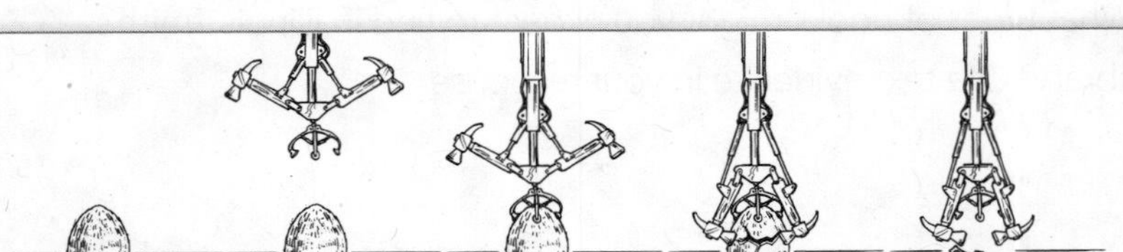

Respond to Questions

These questions will help you think about the sources you've read. Use your notes and refer to the sources to answer the questions. Your answers will help you write your story.

1. What is a Rube Goldberg machine?
   - **a.** an actual machine that Rube Goldberg built
   - **b.** a machine that does a simple thing in a complicated way
   - **c.** a huge suit of armor worn by the French
   - **d.** a room in Illinois Smith's house

2. Which sentence from Source 1 best supports your answer to question 1?
   - **a.** "The English army . . . didn't have such heavy armor . . ."
   - **b.** ". . . had many steps, involving a bird, a clock, and a rocket."
   - **c.** "I have books about everything I collect . . ."
   - **d.** ". . . he offers tours on the third Saturday of every month."

3. What is one similarity in the way both sources present information?
   - **a.** Both talk about Illinois Smith's character.
   - **b.** Both include a conversation with Illinois Smith.
   - **c.** Both convey information about Illinois Smith's home.
   - **d.** Both tell a story about exploring Illinois Smith's house.

4 What is one way "An Adventure Right Here in Lawndale" presents information differently from "The Home of Illinois Smith?"

a. It explains the contents of the rooms in greater detail.

b. It mentions the garden.

c. It talks about Illinois Smith's neighbors.

d. It talks about the secret passageway.

5 **Prose Constructed-Response** In source 1, which details from Illinois Smith's description help the reader visualize the hallway? Use text evidence in your response.

6 **Prose Constructed-Response** What does Source 2 add to your understanding of Illinois Smith's house? Use text evidence in your response.

7 **Prose Constructed-Response** What might be a good hiding spot for someone in Illinois Smith's house? Use text evidence in your response.

Write the Story

Read the assignment.

Assignment
Illinois Smith asks you to watch the house overnight while he is off on another trip. Write a narrative about what happens when you realize you are not alone in the house.

Plan

Use the graphic organizer to help you outline the structure of your narrative.

Introduction

◀ Establish the setting and characters. Alternatively, you may want to jump right into the action. (If so, make sure you introduce setting and characters at some point.)

Event

◀ Develop the plot with a series of events.

Event

Event

Ending

◀ The ending should wrap up the story and resolve the plot.

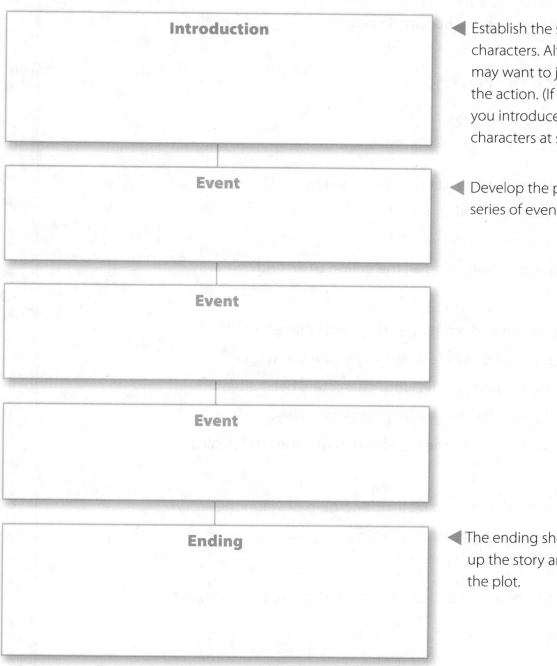

Draft

Use your notes and completed graphic organizer to write a first draft of your narrative.

Revise and Edit

Look back over your story and compare it to the Evaluation Criteria. Revise your story and edit it to correct spelling, grammar, and punctuation errors.

You may wish to draft and edit your story on the computer.

Evaluation Criteria

Your teacher will be looking for:

1. *Organization*
   - Does the introduction get the reader's attention?
   - Is the sequence of events clear?
   - Did you use connecting words?
   - Does the conclusion bring all the action to an end?
2. *Descriptions*
   - Is it clear where and when the story takes place?
   - Do your descriptions help a reader picture the setting?
   - Do descriptive details make your characters believable?
   - Does each character have a distinct personality?
   - Did you use facts from the sources to make the story realistic?
3. *Dialogue*
   - Does the dialogue sound realistic and help develop the story?
   - Is it clear which character is speaking?
4. *Conventions*
   - Did you use proper punctuation, capitalization, and spelling?

On Your Own

Unit 5

Mixed Practice

Task 1

Research Simulation

Opinion Essay

Should students be assigned summer reading?

Task 2

Research Simulation

Informative Essay

Why do people value precious metals and gemstones?

Task 3

Response to Literature

How do different characters each view the events in the story?

Task 4

Research Simulation

Narrative

What happens to a traveler who arrives in the wrong city?

Task **1** **Mixed Practice**

Research Simulation

Opinion Essay

Your Assignment

You will read two texts on summer reading. Then you will write an opinion essay about whether students should be assigned summer reading.

Time Management: Opinion Essay Task

There are two parts to most formal writing tests. Both parts of the tests are timed, so it's important to use your limited time wisely.

Part 1: Read Sources

35

35 minutes! That's not much time.

Preview the Assignment

35 minutes

You will have 35 minutes to read two texts about whether students should be assigned summer reading. You will then answer questions about the sources.

Preview the questions. This will help you know which information you'll need to find as you read.

How Many?

How many pages of reading? ______

How many multiple-choice questions? ______

How many prose constructed-response questions? ______

Underline and take notes as you read. You probably won't have time to reread.

How do you plan to use the 35 minutes?

This is a lot to do in a short time.

Estimated time to read:		
"Summer Is for Relaxing, Not Reading"	______	minutes
"Summer Reading Serves Students"	______	minutes
Estimated time to answer questions?	______	minutes
Total	**35**	**minutes**

Part 2: Write the Essay

85

How much time do you have? Pay attention to the clock!

Plan and Write an Opinion Essay

85 minutes

You will have 85 minutes to plan, write, revise, and edit your essay.

Your Plan

Before you start to write, decide on your opinion. Then think about the reasons and evidence you will use to support your opinion.

How do you plan to use the 85 minutes?

Estimated time for planning the essay?	___ minutes
Estimated time for writing?	___ minutes
Estimated time for editing?	___ minutes
Estimated time for checking spelling, grammar, and punctuation?	___ minutes
Total	**85 minutes**

Be sure to leave enough time for this step!

Reread your essay, making sure that the points are clear. Check that there are no spelling or punctuation mistakes.

Your Assignment

You will read two texts and then write an opinion essay about whether or not students should have summer reading.

Complete the following steps as you plan and compose your essay.

1. Read an editorial about why students should have summer reading.
2. Read an editorial about why students shouldn't have summer reading.
3. Answer questions about the sources.
4. Plan, write, and revise your essay.

Part 1 (35 minutes)

You will now read the sources. Take notes on important facts and details as you read. You can refer to the sources and your notes as you write your essay.

Summer Is for Relaxing, Not Reading

By Ameer Bitar

Students really shouldn't have to complete summer reading. It's sometimes called "required reading," but who wants to be required to do something on vacation? The summer months are supposed to be a time for relaxation and fun. So, summer reading has got to go.

Everybody wants students to read more, and encouraging them to read is part of the reason why summer reading is assigned. But making reading a requirement takes the fun out of it. A book is more fun to read if the reader chooses it. When there is no choice, reading feels more like a chore and less like an opportunity to travel to a different world through words.

Some students might not even read the assigned books all the way through. If they leave assigned reading until the last minute, they will be racing to finish. Maybe they won't complete reading a book, maybe they will skim

Notes

Notes

through the book, or maybe they will just give up on the assignment entirely. One thing is for sure: they will not take the time to appreciate what they are reading. It will just be something to get out of the way. Forcing students to rush through a classic novel isn't a great idea. Letting them read and enjoy it at their leisure makes much more sense.

Students who spend time on assigned summer reading may not have time to read other books that they would choose for themselves. So, the assignment actually discourages a love of reading. When assigned summer reading takes up all of a student's reading time, there may be no energy or desire left for exploring other books.

Some students may not want to complete the assigned reading, or they may decide to read other books instead. This can become a source of tension. Parents shouldn't have to monitor their children's progress with summer reading throughout the vacation. That isn't fun for anyone.

Reading assigned titles is homework, and homework should be limited to times when school is in session.

Am I on Track?

Actual Time Spent Reading

Summer Reading Serves Students

By Cheryl Perlas

Summer reading is important! Students should not have a big interruption in their reading practice. Studies have shown that those who don't read during summer break may see a drop in their reading ability. Coming back to school after the summer can be a real challenge for students who have fallen behind in reading.

When students' reading skills have dropped during the summer, there will be gap between those in the classroom who have maintained their reading level and those who have not. If students read for only 30 minutes a day during the summer they will avoid falling behind. Compared to the homework they have during the school year—after being in school all day—that is a piece of cake! Students who read over the summer may even increase their reading ability, rather than just maintaining their current capability.

Summer reading takes the pressure off! Students have more time to read, and they don't have other homework to worry about. If there isn't as much to do in a day, more time can be spent paying attention to the books that they are reading.

Reading is a lot of fun. When students read a book on a required reading list, it can spark an interest in finding out more about a topic or reading another book by the same

Notes

Notes

author. Students who don't have to read these assigned titles may never know what they are missing. Summer reading is a great opportunity for students to find out where their interests lie.

Reading can be done almost anywhere. Students can read in the park, at the beach, on the subway, or even in the bathtub! If they are reading to find out information, they can complete assigned reading by listening to an audiobook. There is no need to sit still for long periods of time. An audiobook on an mp3 player lets a student listen while riding a bike or walking to a friend's house. It doesn't even have to interfere with many other things the student wants to do.

Some schools provide a list of books, and students choose the titles they want to read. In this case, the school will tell the students how many titles to pick. This allows the students to choose titles or topics that they find interesting. Other schools give students a fixed list of books to read. This means students can reach out to classmates to discuss the assigned books.

Most school subjects require reading skills. Everyday life requires reading skills. Most jobs require reading skills. An ideal way to encourage students to improve their reading skills is to let them choose from a wide variety of good books. That way, summer reading is rewarding and enjoyable.

Am I on Track?

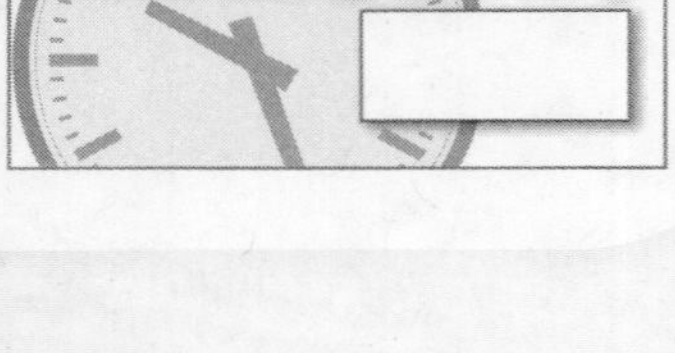

Questions

Answer the following questions. You may refer to your reading notes, and you should cite text evidence in your responses. Your answers to these questions will be scored. You will be able to refer to your answers as you write your essay in Part 2.

1. The word *skim* is used in the source called "Summer Is for Relaxing, Not Reading." What choice has the same meaning as *skim*?

   a. read

   b. cut off

   c. sleep

   d. look over

2. **Prose Constructed-Response** According to "Summer Is for Relaxing, Not Reading," how can assigned summer reading be unhelpful to students?

3. **Prose Constructed-Response** In "Summer Reading Serves Students," how can summer reading encourage students to read more?

Part 2 (85 minutes)

You now have 85 minutes to review your notes and sources and to plan, draft, revise, and edit your essay. While you may use your notes and refer to the sources, your essay must represent your original work. You may refer to your responses to the questions in Part 1, but you cannot change those answers. Now read your assignment and begin your work.

Your assignment

You have read two sources about summer reading. Each text discusses whether students should be assigned summer reading. The two texts are:

- "Summer Is for Relaxing, Not Reading"
- "Summer Reading Serves Students"

Consider the opinions presented in the texts on whether students should be assigned summer reading.

Write an essay that gives your opinion on whether students should be assigned summer reading. Remember to use reasons and evidence to support your opinion.

Now begin work on your essay. Manage your time carefully so that you can:

1. plan your essay
2. write your essay
3. revise and edit your final draft

Task 2 **Mixed Practice**

Research Simulation

Informative Essay

Your Assignment

You will read two texts about precious metals and gemstones. Then, you will write an informative essay about the reasons people value these materials.

Time Management: Informative Essay Task

Most formal writing tests are made up of two parts. Both parts of the tests are timed, so it's important to use your limited time wisely.

Part 1: Read Sources

35

35 minutes! That's not much time.

Preview the Assignment

35 minutes

You will have 35 minutes to read two selections about precious metals and gemstones. You will then answer questions about the sources.

Preview the questions. This will help you know which information you'll need to find as you read.

How Many?

How many pages of reading? ____

How many multiple-choice questions? ____

How many prose constructed-response questions? ____

Underline and take notes as you read. You probably won't have time to reread.

How do you plan to use the 35 minutes?

This is a lot to do in a short time.

Estimated time to read:

"Why It's Worth What It's Worth" ____ minutes

"It Does More than Glitter" ____ minutes

Estimated time to answer questions? ____ minutes

Total **35 minutes**

Part 2: Write the Essay

How much time do you have? Pay attention to the clock!

Plan and Write an Informative Essay

85 minutes

You will have 85 minutes to plan, write, revise, and edit your essay.

Your Plan

Before you start to write, decide on a main idea for your essay and details that support your main idea.

How do you plan to use the 85 minutes?

Be sure to leave enough time for this step!

Estimated time for planning the essay?	____ minutes
Estimated time for writing?	____ minutes
Estimated time for editing?	____ minutes
Estimated time for checking spelling, grammar, and punctuation?	____ minutes
Total	**85 minutes**

Reread your essay, making sure that the points are clear. Check that there are no spelling or punctuation mistakes.

Your Assignment

You will read two texts about precious metals and gemstones. Then, you will write an informative essay about the reasons people value these materials.

Complete the following steps as you plan and compose your essay.

1. Read an informational article about why precious metals and gemstones are expensive.
2. Read an informational article about the physical properties of gold, silver, and diamonds.
3. Answer questions about the sources.
4. Plan, write, and revise your essay.

Part 1 (35 minutes)

You will now read the sources. Take notes on important facts and details as you read. You can refer to the sources and your notes as you write your essay.

Why It's Worth What It's Worth

by Gerald Fring

In 2013, the "Pink Star," a diamond weighing less than half an ounce, sold at auction for 72 million dollars. That same year, the average price for an ounce of gold was 1,464 dollars. Gemstones such as diamonds, rubies and sapphires, and precious metals such as gold and silver, cost a lot of money. Why is this? There are two properties that all these things have in common: beauty and scarcity.

Many people find gold beautiful because of its warm shine. Gold never rusts or tarnishes the way some other metals do, so even gold jewelry from thousands of years ago still looks the way it did when it was made. Gold is also very rare—all of the gold humans have refined in the world could fit into a cube 20 meters on a side.

When it's polished, silver is one of the world's shiniest metals. This means that it reflects the most light. However, it tarnishes quickly if you don't polish it. This, combined

Notes

Notes

with the fact that silver is more common than gold, makes it less valuable. Gold and silver are the two most workable metals. They can easily be shaped into coins, jewelry and other objects that have value.

Gemstones such as emeralds and sapphires are expensive because of their beauty and scarcity. Rubies (which are really red sapphires) are even more valuable. But perhaps the most valued gemstone of all is the diamond. Light that enters a cut diamond bends and reflects, causing that special sparkle that people prize so much. And, like sapphires, diamonds also come in a variety of colors. The dark-blue Hope Diamond, the Moussaieff Red Diamond, and the Pink Star are examples of famous colored diamonds.

Diamonds are very rare. They were formed deep in the earth under high pressure and heat. Then, volcanic eruptions moved them closer to the earth's surface. And then, people searched for them in mines. When you also consider the fact that most diamonds are over a billion years old, you can start to realize just why they cost so much.

So, a combination of rarity and beauty makes materials expensive. In the 19th century, aluminum was so rare and valuable that the emperor of France only let his special guests use his set of aluminum knives and forks, while other guests had to settle for gold. But once scientists discovered an easy way to refine aluminum, its value vanished almost overnight. Now it's in everything from baseball bats to soda cans. Would the same thing happen to gold, silver, and gemstones if we could find them as easily as aluminum?

Am I on Track?

It Does More than Glitter

by Gabriela Castillo

Notes

More than 2,000 years ago, the Greeks and Chinese discovered that magnetite, a mineral, has a special property. It attracts iron. This property led to magnetite's use in the compass, which hugely changed exploration and navigation. It goes without saying that people use materials because of their characteristics. The value of many materials also depends on their usefulness. Some materials that are highly-valued for their beauty and scarcity also very desirable physical properties.

Gold is worth its weight in . . . well, gold! It's very expensive. Aside from it's beauty as a metal, it has properties that give it many practical uses. Gold is a very good conductor of electricity and it doesn't corrode over time. That makes it essential in computer chips, cell phones, and many other electronic devices. It's easy to work with, which makes it great as a dental filling for

Notes

fixing cavities. Farther from home, spacecraft are covered with a gold skin that reflects radiation and keeps the craft from getting too hot.

Another precious metal, silver, is one of the most reflective. Sheets of glass coated with silver make excellent mirrors. This metal also interferes with the ways bacteria keep themselves alive, so it is effective as an antibiotic. Throughout history, people kept water in silver containers to kill off germs that caused diseases. At the beginning of the 20th century, people even put silver coins into their milk bottles to keep the milk fresh for longer periods of time.

Diamond is another expensive substance that isn't just for jewelry. The word diamond comes from a Greek word meaning "unbreakable." It's a fitting name—diamond is the hardest known natural material on Earth. In fact, the only thing that can cut a diamond is another diamond. Diamonds can withstand extreme pressure and heat, so they are commonly used in many industries. Diamond dust or small stones are used to coat drill bits, grinding wheels, rock saws, lathes, and glass cutters. Special scalpels made with diamond are also used by doctors to make very fine cuts during delicate surgeries.

Gold, silver, and diamond are just three examples of expensive and useful materials. The next time you admire a beautiful piece of jewelry, remember that its materials are valuable in many ways.

Am I on Track?

Actual Time Spent Reading

Questions

Answer the following questions. You may refer to your reading notes. Your answers to these questions will be scored. You will be able to refer to your answers as you write your essay in Part 2.

1. The word *antibiotic* is used in the source "It Does More than Glitter." What word has the same meaning as *antibiotic*?

   a. obstacle

   b. bacteria-killing

   c. freshness

   d. history

2. Which choice best helps the reader understand the meaning of *antibiotic*?

   a. ". . . people even put silver coins into their milk bottles to keep the milk fresh . . ."

   b. "Sheets of glass coated with silver make excellent mirrors."

   c. "Gold, silver, and diamond are just three examples of expensive and useful materials."

   d. "This metal also interferes with the ways bacteria keep themselves alive . . ."

3. Which of the following claims could one make after reading these selections?

   a. Gold is worth less than silver because it is more common and tarnishes more easily.

   b. The only thing that makes diamonds valuable is their extreme hardness.

   c. The rarity of natural diamonds is an important reason they cost so much.

   d. The rarity of precious metals and stones has little to do with their value.

Part 2 (85 minutes)

You now have 85 minutes to review your notes and sources and to plan, draft, revise, and edit your essay. While you may use your notes and refer to the sources, your essay must represent your original work. You may refer to your responses to the questions in Part 1, but you cannot change those answers. Now read your assignment and begin your work.

Your assignment

You have read two sources about precious metals and stones.

The two texts are:

- "Why It's Worth What It's Worth"
- "It Does More than Glitter"

Think about the information regarding precious metals and stones as it is presented in both texts.

Write an essay that explains why people value precious metals and gemstones. Remember to use textual evidence to develop your topic.

Now begin work on your essay. Manage your time carefully so that you can:

1. plan your essay
2. write your essay
3. revise and edit your final draft

Response to Literature

Your Assignment

You will read the Korean folk tale "The Pheasant's Bell." Then you will use what you have read to write a response to literature comparing the characters' view of events in a story.

Time Management: Response to Literature Task

There are two parts to most formal writing tests. Both parts of the tests are timed, so it's important to use your limited time wisely.

Part 1: Read the Source

35

35 minutes! That's not much time.

Preview the Assignment

35 minutes

You will have 35 minutes to read the Korean folk tale "The Pheasant's Bell." You will then answer questions about the source.

Preview the questions. This will help you know which information you'll need to find as you read.

How Many?

How many pages of reading? ____

How many multiple-choice questions? ____

How many prose constructed-response questions? ____

Underline and take notes as you read. You probably won't have time to reread.

How do you plan to use the 35 minutes?

This is a lot to do in a short time.

Estimated time to read: "The Pheasant's Bell" ____ minutes

Estimated time to answer questions? ____ minutes

Total **35 minutes**

Part 2: Write the Essay

85

How much time do you have? Pay attention to the clock!

Plan and Write a Response to Literature

85 minutes

You will have 85 minutes to plan, write, revise, and edit your response to literature.

Your Plan

Before you start to write, determine the main idea of your response to literature and the details that support your main idea.

How do you plan to use the 85 minutes?

Be sure to leave enough time for this step!

Estimated time for planning the essay?		minutes
Estimated time for writing?		minutes
Estimated time for editing?		minutes
Estimated time for checking spelling, grammar, and punctuation?		minutes
Total	**85**	**minutes**

Reread your essay, making sure that the points are clear. Check that there are no spelling or punctuation mistakes.

Your Assignment

> You will read a text and then write a response to literature comparing how different characters view the events in the story.

Complete the following steps as you plan and compose your essay.

1. Read "The Pheasant's Bell."
2. Answer questions about the source.
3. Plan, write, and revise your response to literature.

Part 1 (35 minutes)

You will now read the source. Take notes on important details as you read. You can refer to the source and your notes as you write your essay.

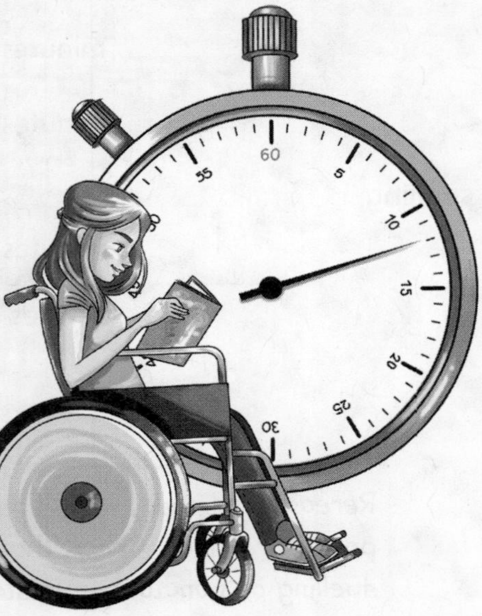

"The Pheasant's Bell"

Retold by Kim So-un

Deep in a lonely forest there once lived a woodcutter. One day the woodcutter was at work felling trees, when he heard the cry of a pheasant and the fluttering of wings nearby. He wondered what was happening and went to see what the commotion was about. Under the shade of a bush he saw a pheasant nest with many eggs inside it. A great snake was poised to strike at a mother pheasant, who was bravely trying to defend her nest. The woodcutter picked up a stick and tried to scare the snake away, crying: "Go away! Go away!" But the snake wouldn't move, so the woodcutter struck it with his stick and killed it.

Some years after this, the woodcutter one day set out on a distant journey. Twilight found him walking along a lonely mountain path. Soon it became completely dark. He was hungry and tired. Suddenly, far ahead of him in

Notes

Notes

the woods he saw a dim light. He walked toward this light and came to a large and beautiful straw-thatched house. The woodcutter was surprised, for he had never expected to find such a fine house so deep in the forest. He knocked on the door, and a beautiful girl, about nineteen or twenty years of age, came out.

"I am hungry and tired," the woodcutter told her. "I have walked a long way today and have no place to stay. I wonder if you would put me up for the night?"

The girl answered in a kind tone: "I am alone in this house, but please do come in."

She welcomed the woodcutter inside and spread out a grand feast for him. But the woodcutter felt very ill at ease. He could not understand why such a beautiful young girl should be living all alone in the middle of a forest. He couldn't help wondering if he hadn't entered a haunted house. But he was so hungry that he ate the fine food put before him and asked no questions. Only when he was quite full did he finally speak.

"Why should such a young person as you live all alone here in such a large house?" he asked.

"I am waiting to take my revenge against my enemy," the girl answered.

"Your enemy?" he asked. "Where would he be?"

"He is right here," she said. "See, you are my enemy!" Then she opened a great red mouth and laughed loudly.

The woodcutter was astounded and asked her why he should be her enemy.

The girl reminded him of the time he had saved the mother pheasant and her nest, and added: "I am the snake

Notes

you killed that time. I've waited a long long time to meet up with you. And now I'm going to take your life. Then finally I'll have the revenge I've dreamed of so long."

When the woodcutter heard this, his heart sank. "I had nothing against you at that time," he said in a quavering voice. "It was simply because I couldn't bear to see helpless beings hurt by someone strong like you were. That's why I saved the pheasant. But I really didn't mean to kill you. Don't say I'm your enemy. Please, please spare my life."

At first the girl kept laughing at him and would not listen to his pleas. But he kept on pleading, from bended knees, with tears flowing down his cheeks.

"All right then," the girl said, "I'll give you one chance. Deep in the forest and high in the mountains there is a temple ruin. Not a single soul lives there. However, a huge bell hangs in that temple. If, before dawn, you are able to ring that bell without moving from the place where you're sitting now, then I'll spare your life."

When the woodcutter heard this, he was even more frightened. "How can I ring that bell while I'm still sitting here in this room?" he sighed. "You're unfair. I'm no better off than before. Please don't say such a cruel thing. It's the same as killing me right now. Please let me go home."

The girl firmly refused: "No! You are the enemy I've waited for so long. Yes, I've waited a long time for this chance to avenge myself. Now that I have you in my hands, why should I let you go? If you can't ring the bell, resign yourself to death. I shall eat you up."

The woodcutter gave up all hope. He realized that he was as good as dead.

Notes

Suddenly, the quiet night air vibrated with the sound of a distant bell. "Bong!" the bell rang. Yes, it was the bell in the crumbling old mountain temple!

When the girl heard the bell, she turned white and gnashed her teeth. "It's no use," she said. "You must be guarded by the gods."

No sooner had she said this than she disappeared from sight. The fine house in which the woodcutter was sitting also disappeared in a puff of smoke.

The woodcutter, whose life had been so miraculously saved, could hardly wait for daylight to break. With the first sign of dawn he set off toward the mountains in search of the ruined temple, filled with gnawing curiosity.

Sure enough, as he had been told, there he found a temple in which hung a great bell. But there was not a single soul in sight. The woodcutter looked at the bell in wonder. On it he noticed a stain of blood. He looked down to the floor. There, with head shattered and wings broken, lay the blood-stained body of a pheasant.

Am I on Track?

Actual Time Spent Reading

Questions

Answer the following questions. You may refer to your reading notes, and you should cite text evidence in your responses. Your answers to these questions will be scored. You will be able to refer to your answers as you write your essay in Part 2.

1. The word *avenge* is used in line 71. What choice has the same meaning as *avenge*?

   a. wait

   b. kill

   c. let go

   d. get even

2. **Prose Constructed-Response** Why does the pheasant help the woodcutter?

   ____

   ____

   ____

   ____

3. **Prose Constructed-Response** How do the viewpoints of the snake and the woodcutter differ about the reason why the woodcutter killed the snake?

   ____

   ____

   ____

   ____

Part 2 (85 minutes)

You now have 85 minutes to review your notes and the source and to plan, draft, revise, and edit your essay. While you may use your notes and refer to the source, your essay must represent your original work. You may refer to your responses to the questions in Part 1, but you cannot change those answers. Now read your assignment and begin your work.

Your assignment

You have read "The Pheasant's Bell."

Write a response to literature comparing how the woodcutter, the snake, and the pheasant view the events in the story.

Now begin work on your essay. Manage your time carefully so that you can:

1. plan your essay
2. write your essay
3. revise and edit your final draft

Task 4 **Mixed Practice**

Research Simulation

Narrative

Your Assignment

You will read two texts, each about a city called Athens. Then you will write a narrative about what happens when a traveler who wants to fly to Athens, Georgia, accidentally arrives in Athens, Greece.

Time Management: Narrative Task

Most formal writing tests are made up of two parts. Both parts of the tests are timed, so it's important to use your limited time wisely.

Part 1: Read Sources

35

35 minutes! That's not much time.

Preview the Assignment

35 minutes

You will have 35 minutes to read two selections about two cities named Athens. You will then answer questions about the sources.

Preview the questions. This will help you know which information you'll need to find as you read.

How Many?

How many pages of reading? ☐

How many multiple-choice questions? ☐

How many prose constructed-response questions? ☐

Underline and take notes as you read. You probably won't have time to reread.

How do you plan to use the 35 minutes?

This is a lot to do in a short time.

Estimated time to read:

"Welcome to Athens, Georgia!" ☐ minutes

"Come Home to Athens" ☐ minutes

Estimated time to answer questions? ☐ minutes

Total **35 minutes**

Part 2: Write the Narrative

85

How much time do you have? Pay attention to the clock!

Plan and Write a Narrative

85 minutes

You will have 85 minutes to plan, write, revise, and edit your story.

Your Plan

Before you start to write, determine the information from the sources you will use as a basis for your story. Then decide what will happen in your story.

How do you plan to use the 85 minutes?

Be sure to leave enough time for this step!

Estimated time for planning the story?	____ minutes
Estimated time for writing?	____ minutes
Estimated time for editing?	____ minutes
Estimated time for checking spelling, grammar, and punctuation?	____ minutes
Total	**85 minutes**

Reread your story, making sure that the points are clear. Check that there are no spelling or punctuation mistakes.

Your Assignment

> You will read two texts and then write a narrative about what happens when a traveler who wants to fly to Athens, Georgia, accidentally arrives in Athens, Greece.

Complete the following steps as you plan and compose your narrative.

1. Read an informational article about Athens, Georgia.
2. Read an informational article about Athens, Greece.
3. Answer questions about the sources.
4. Plan, write, and revise your story.

Part 1 (35 minutes)

You will now read the sources. Take notes on important facts and details as you read. You can refer to the sources and your notes as you write your story.

Welcome to Athens, Georgia!

Athens is a city of about 120,000 people in northern Georgia. When it first became a town, there were 17 families living there, but it was already the home of America's first state college. Athens still has a college-town feel—it is in a great location and has a long history, affordable rents, and plenty of culture.

One of the first things visitors notice about Athens is that it's a friendly city. The population represents a mix of ages and cultures. Downtown is a historic district where the buildings are preserved; the streets are people-friendly and bike-friendly.

The area around the college and downtown is packed with theaters, galleries, and restaurants. The city is home to two famous museums—the Georgia Museum of Natural History and the Georgia Museum of Art. The State Botanical Garden of Georgia covers more than 300 acres and includes amazing displays of rare and exotic plants as well as miles of nature trails.

Aside from its fame as a beautiful city with a pleasant climate, Athens is world-renowned as a center for music. Many famous bands found their start there, and there are numerous opportunities to see stars and upcoming performers every evening.

Notes

Am I on Track?

Actual Time Spent Reading

Notes

Come Home to Athens

Athens is considered the birthplace of western civilization—the city invented democracy! It has over 5,000 years of history, and a lot of it is still on display. Every year, three million visitors marvel at the massive temples that were built 2,500 years ago on the Acropolis, a rocky outcrop rising above the city. Just as many people visit the National Archaeological Museum of Athens, the most important museum in the world devoted to ancient Greek art.

Walking is the best way to see most of the city's major archaeological sites—theaters, arches, the market place. In fact, a pedestrian walkway goes through the historical district and passes almost all of them.

Downtown Athens has amazing old buildings, too, but these are from the 1800s and early 1900s. However, the city doesn't live in the past. Nestled among the important architecture are modern shops, restaurants, and movie theaters.

Athens would be a fabulous city even in the fog and rain, but the weather is sunny and warm year-round. And a 45-minute ride on the train or bus will take you to a beach on the Aegean sea.

Am I on Track?

Actual Time Spent Reading

Questions

Answer the following questions. You may refer to your reading notes, and you should cite text evidence in your responses. Your answers to these questions will be scored. You will be able to refer to your answers as you write your story in Part 2.

1. According to the sources, which of the following statements is a fact about both Athens, Georgia, and Athens, Greece?
   - **a.** Both cities are bike-friendly.
   - **b.** They each have a historical district.
   - **c.** Both cities are close to the ocean.
   - **d.** They are both college towns.

2. **Prose Constructed-Response** Explain whether the climate in Athens, Greece is similar to the climate in Athens, Georgia.

____

____

____

____

3. **Prose Constructed-Response** How might the way you spend your days in Athens, Greece, differ from those in Athens, Georgia?

____

____

____

____

____

Part 2 (85 minutes)

You now have 85 minutes to review your notes and the sources and to plan, draft, revise, and edit your narrative. While you may use your notes and refer to the source, your story must represent your original work. You may refer to your responses to the questions in Part 1, but you cannot change those answers. Now read your assignment and begin your work.

Your assignment

You have read two sources about two different cities, each named Athens. The two texts are:

- "Welcome to Athens, Georgia!"
- "Come Home to Athens"

Write a narrative about a plane ticket mix-up. A traveler bought a plane ticket to Athens, Georgia, but arrived in Athens, Greece.

Now begin work on your narrative. Manage your time carefully so that you can:

1. plan your story

2. write your story

3. revise and edit your final draft

Acknowledgments

"The Pheasant's Bell" from *The Story Bag* by Kim So-un, translated by Setsu Higashi. Text copyright © 1955 by Charles E. Tuttle Co., Inc. Reprinted by permission of Tuttle Publishing.

The True Story of the Three Little Pigs! by Jon Scieszka, illustrated by Lane Smith. Text copyright © 1989 by Jon Scieszka. Illustrations copyright © 1989 by Lane Smith. Reprinted by permission of Viking Penguin, a division of Penguin Group (USA) LLC.

Two Bad Ants by Chris Van Allsburg. Copyright © 1988 by Chris Van Allsburg. Reprinted by permission of Houghton Mifflin Harcourt Publishing Company.